THE SPARKLE

YOU ARE MORE THAN
WHAT YOU HAVE BECOME

ROBIN KIRBY

Sparkle House Press

Sparkle House
Press

For everyone on the edge of burnout who knows there has to be more.

To my younger self who was too stubborn to listen.

To my future self that will need to hear it again.

Copyright © 2023 by Robin Kirby

The Sparkle by Robin Kirby

DISCLAIMER

Although this publication is designed to provide accurate information in regard to the subject matter covered, the publisher and the author assume no responsibility for errors, inaccuracies, omissions, or any other inconsistencies herein. This publication is meant as a source of valuable information for the reader, however it is not meant as a replacement for direct expert assistance. If such level of assistance is required, the services of a competent professional should be sought.

Printed by Sparkle House Press, 2023, First Printing
sparklehousepress@gmail.com

Book template by Used to Tech (https://usedtotech.com)
Cover Photo: By Morgan Sessions on Unsplash.com

First Printing Edition, 2023
ISBN #: 979-8-9875586-0-7

Table of Contents

SECTION 1: THE BASELINE

Introduction...1

Chapter 1: Check Engine Lights...................................5

Chapter 2: A Gut Check...13

SECTION 2: GETTING ACCURATE

Chapter 3: Recalculating...31

Chapter 4: The Recipe...39

SECTION 3: "U"-TELLIGENCE

Chapter 5: Your Inventory...47

Chapter 6: Your Definition..55

Chapter 7: Your Reflections.......................................63

Chapter 8: Your Values..69

Chapter 9: Your Personality & Career Options............75

Chapter 10: Your Superpower....................................89

Chapter 11: Your Allergies...97

Chapter 12: Your Currency......................................105

SECTION 4: POWER TOOLS

Chapter 13: Knowledge: Sparkle Sources 115

Chapter 14: Knowledge: Sparkle Stealers 125

Chapter 15: Power Tool: Rest...151

Chapter 16: Power Tools: Questions & Boundaries 165

Chapter 17: Power Tool: Systems 173

Chapter 18: Power Tools: Plans and Goals..179

SECTION 5: MAKING IT REAL

Chapter 19: Power Tool: Role Models - Real Life Sparklers 197

Chapter 20: It Is Time 207

APPENDIX

Appendix A: Spiritual Rest..216

Appendix B: Core Values 227

SECTION I

THE BASELINE

INTRODUCTION

If you let it, this book can change your life.

If you are achingly exhausted, chronically cranky, on the razor's edge of burnout, and just trying to "keep it together," this book is for you.

If you feel more like acid rain and tornado than sunshine and rainbows, this is for you.

If you are 25, 45, or anywhere in between and still trying to find a career that lights you up, this book is for you.

If you are tired of hustling for your worthiness at work or trying to "fake it till you make it," this is for you.

If you feel lost, empty, confused about your career, stuck, frozen in place, or are chasing someone else's dream, this book is for you.

If you shrink more than you shine, if you worry more than you wonder and if your soul silently shouts, "there has to be more," this is for you.

*****

I know it's for you because I was you. I was all of those things. I was physically and mentally present for a job that I was a thousand miles away from emotionally. It gave me money and status but took my joy and every minute of my time in exchange. I was endlessly irritated, huffingly impatient, clinically cynical and in the clutches of soul-crippling burnout.

So it's ironic that I'm writing a book called The Sparkle three years later. If you asked a friend to describe me back then, I doubt that "sparkly" would have been anywhere on their list. Hard-charging, busy, successful, no-nonsense, overwhelmed, and annoyed would have been better candidates for the list.

Without knowing it, the old Robin was in survival mode and was in a battle with a life that I thankfully would lose. Life physically knocked me to the ground, looked deep into my eyes, and said, "Pay attention, stop this madness, or I'll do it for you. You were not designed for this and you are more than what you have become."

So, for the first time in my life, I listened. I stopped in my tracks and made a 180-degree turn in my life and career. I began a transformation that would unlock a part of me I didn't know I had. Now, I have a life full of joy, energy, and freedom. I have a life full of flow, possibility, meaning, and impact. There is a spring in my step, and a sparkle in my eye that I didn't know existed. I want to help you have it too.

The idea for this book came out of a LinkedIn™ blog post that I wrote that completely shocked me. I wrote the blog to update all my working world friends about what I was doing. As part of my transformation, I had quit a high-visibility job a year prior and had not yet returned to the corporate world. Friends and acquaintances were wondering what was going on.

The Robin they knew would only have left a job because she had a better, more high-paying, bigger job lined up. In contrast, this Robin turned down recruiter calls and instead called her friends to just say Hi. That was not like the old Robin.

So, I started writing an update, and the words flowed like water. I cannot describe how quickly and easily they came onto the page or how exhilarating it felt while I was writing. I was in a zone, and it was the therapy that I didn't even know I needed. I wrote a quick version and surprised myself at how vulnerable and honest the words were. I was an introvert who rarely posted on social media, and now I was baring my soul to 2,000 of my closest LinkedIn™ friends.

The old Robin, at all costs, kept up a façade that her corporate career was wonderful and that she had made something of herself. While some of that was true, what was also true was that I no longer recognized who I was or liked what I saw in the mirror. It was time for a change, and without knowing it, this was my debut. I remember sitting with my finger on the button for an hour before I posted it. I knew my backup plan of going back into the corporate world would be torpedoed with the post. I decided to hit the button anyway.

Ding, ding, ding, da ding, da ding, da ding. My phone began buzzing with new comments and likes minutes after I posted it. Ten thousand views and hundreds of comments, likes, and personal text messages later, I was in near tears. Never in my life had I felt so seen, so heard, and so connected. The messages were humbling. People I had worked with for years were sharing feelings I would never have expected.

Here is a sample:

"I just read your post on The Sparkle, and honestly, I think you touched my soul. Your reflections took me on a journey, and I'm so happy for you. I've forgotten about my sparkle with everything life has thrown at me, but I think I'm going to change some perspectives after this."

"I've read this more than a handful of times, sent it to some close friends, and quoted pieces aloud to my family at dinner last night. It spurred thinking and dialogue around our definitions of success and understanding the obstacles between our lives now and those definitions."

"Just had to say - wow!!!! On your blog!!! Honestly, your description of the corporate experience was what I felt and still feel about that time. It took my breath away. Imagine if we had all talked about that reality then??"

People were connecting to a raw honesty about the hidden questions and emotions we all feel. Feelings about purpose, definitions of success, ambitions, and our working lives. Emotions about a desire to recapture something they, like me, had lost...their sparkle. So, *The Sparkle* was born. I am passionate now about helping you feel this exhilaration and to feel your heart and brain sparkle again (or maybe for the first time).

This book takes an honest, sometimes edgy, look at ourselves, our working world, our time, and how we spend it. It will take you on a journey into yourself. It will teach you how to find your sparkle, keep it, and be a spark to others in the working world. I want to shower you with love, truth, grace, and knowledge to help you unlock the bright and joyous future that is waiting for you.

That said, please know that I am not a counselor nor a medical or mental health practitioner. Nothing I say should be taken as advice in these areas. This book is simply based on my decades of living and breathing this firsthand in my own personal and professional life.

I want to help you find your blue flame, that elusive intersection of your passion, purpose, and ability. I want you to live a life where work is effortless, and joy is endless. It is an incredible place to be.

If you are reading these words, you are probably one of the busiest people you know, and time is in short supply. So, I thank you and applaud you for taking this brief moment for yourself. I am a firm believer that knowledge is power. Knowing yourself, knowing what you value, and knowing the type of sparkle you have to offer the working world (and maybe the world) can be life-changing; I know it was for me.

****

CHAPTER 1

CHECK ENGINE LIGHTS

My story to help inspire yours.

Don't let what happened to me to happen to you.

In June of 2019, I had one of the loudest check engine light moments I have ever had, and I missed it. It was a loud, obnoxious, in-your-face, brightly flashing red neon light, and I missed it. I saw it but ignored it. I told it I knew better and missed the message entirely. As a result, I ran headfirst into a complete physical and emotional brick wall that nearly broke every emotional bone I had.

Here is the story.

I was blessed to join a fantastic organization early in my career and was the happiest I had ever been. The culture fit me like a glove, and I was in my zone. The problem was, I was ambitious and always took the Silicon Valley recruiter calls. They were enticing. Big titles, sexy brands, and much bigger pay. Eventually they won and I left a place I loved and a job that lit me up. Little did I know that would be the start of a collision course for me. The ambitious, and if I'm honest, a little greedy version of myself was in her element. I had no idea though what it was truly costing me. If I had only known then what I know now.

THE WHACK

The tipping point started in 2018. I had taken a series of roles that required heavy global travel, including monthly trips to India and weekly commutes to Texas. After flying home from one of these trips, I got into my car, drove home, and did all my usual unpacking and repacking routine. All was normal, except I noticed as I was moving my suitcase around that I was getting increasingly short of breath. I didn't think much of it and thought I was just imagining things, so I went about my day.

The next day, I was out running an errand and noticed I was still out of breath. I happened to look down at my leg and saw that the top of my leg had turned purple, and I knew something was wrong. So, what was the first thing I did? What any self-respecting workaholic would do, of course. I went home, made sure I got out those last emails, and then decided I should go to the emergency room.

Seven hours and multiple tests later, a handsome young doctor came into my room. He said I had one of the most severe cases of blood clots and pulmonary embolisms they had seen, not to mention for someone who was in her early 40s and healthy. I would later learn that I had a perfect storm brewing in my body, and it was not a matter of if, but when this would happen. I had several genetic mutations that triggered clots and was on medication that put me at higher risk. In addition, I was constantly flying and had a recent fall that kept me stationary for long periods. It truly was a perfect storm.

The doctor told me I had an extensive deep vein thrombosis (DVT) in my top right thigh and multiple blood clots in not one but both of my lungs. One of them was near my heart and could be extremely deadly. They immediately put me on a Heparin drip and immobilized me. Any movement could trigger the blood clot to move to my heart, which would be fatal. I was put into the ICU, given some risky but highly effective clot-busting drugs, and taken back to surgery to remove the larger clots.

Gratefully, their extraordinary efforts worked, but I would need a new kind of life from then on. The doctor gave me four discharge instructions:

take blood thinners, reduce or stop my flying, lower my stress levels, and to just live my life. Now there was a challenge if I ever heard one!

For the next few months, I felt entirely out of my element. I was physically grounded for the first time in my life and desperately trying to figure my life out. How would I manage my out-of-state job without being able to fly? How would I stay low-stress in a very high-stress role?

So, I did what I always did. I went into planning and action mode to find a new job instead of going into pause and reflection mode. This would have been a great moment to slow things down and think about what God and my body were trying to tell me. It's too bad slowing down wasn't in my vocabulary.

THE CRASH

It didn't take me long to find a new role. This was all happening in the middle of the chaos of 2020, so I was thankful to find the role and excited about my next chapter. My new company seemed like a fun culture, and the role put me at the top of my career ladder.

The expectations are incredibly high when you are the senior executive HR leader at a publicly traded company. I was at a fast-growth tech company and spent a lot of time with our board and executive team navigating through the complexities of 2020. In addition, the company went through multiple CEO changes in my first year there, which is incredibly stressful for an HR organization.

So here I was, an ambitious workaholic who had already been burnt out already for years, trying to grind my way through it. The first year was a whirlwind of hiring, Covid navigation, board meetings, presentations, and navigating change. I was routinely working 60 to 80 hours a week, and was more stressed than I had ever been because of my own workaholism.

I had personal dreams I could see that were slipping away and relationships that were shrinking due to my neglect. I also knew deep down that I had spent 20 years pursuing a career that did not fit my personality, so there was that.

I was chronically cranky, endlessly irritated, and had less than zero patience. I was a cauldron of frustration mixed with cups of boiling stress and spoonfuls of regret, stirred by a daily dose of chaos. If you had asked those closest to me back then, they might have more accurately described me as a hot mix of acid rain and tornado.

In July of that year, my F5 tornado crashed right into a physical, emotional, and mental wall, and for the first time in my life, I didn't know how to crawl over or punch through it. I had gone in for a routine mammogram, and the results showed something concerning. They told me they wanted me to return in a couple of days and rerun the test to see if they could get a better angle. A younger, less stressed version of myself could have taken that in stride, but I was at a breaking point. I remember getting into the car, calling my husband, and breaking into an uncontrollable 15 minutes of crying and having a mild panic attack.

My poor husband didn't know what to think; this was very unlike me. I was the strong one. I was the one who punched through all the walls. I wasn't the emotional one that was curled up in a puddle on the floor of her front seat, sobbing uncontrollably.

We were right in the middle of a major change initiative. This one was significant and needed a lot of my attention, but I just did not have it to give. I called my boss and told him I needed a couple of days to figure out what was going on and to take a break. I physically and emotionally was in the fetal position and needed time. I prided myself in rarely ever calling in sick and could not have imagined not being there to help lead through this change. The timing could not have been worse, and I was grateful that he was understanding. Luckily, I had an amazing team that could step up and take the reins.

Thankfully, the mammogram scare was a false alarm, but the looming life whack I felt coming during those 48 hours left a mark. It turned my mind into a raging stream of thoughts and emotions that I could no longer hold back. I felt like a broken piece of pottery. Yet amid the brokenness, somewhere in the back of my mind, I remembered a phrase I heard once – "cracks are what let the light in." I was ready to see the light. So I used the time off to do some intense soul-searching and reflecting, the kind that I should have done two years prior.

I took an inventory of my life and decided to get off the corporate treadmill, focus on myself, and find my sparkle again. This was a big deal for me. I had wrapped my entire personal identity and 20 years of my life around climbing this ladder and creating this career, and I was walking away from it. Strangely, I felt complete and utter peace. With every fiber of my being, I knew this was the right call, and there was no changing my mind. So, I turned in my notice and began this incredible journey into finding myself, figuring out what I want to be when I grow up, and finding my sparkle.

I don't want what happened to me to happen to you. I don't want you to have to hit that wall. I don't want you to have to pay a physical, emotional, and mental price that you don't have to pay. I don't want you to sacrifice your relationships and your happiness. I want you to pay attention to your check engine lights.

If your current working circumstances are costing you your physical, emotional, or mental health, it is too expensive. It doesn't have to be this way. I want you to be intentional about your life, and to avoid getting "bumper car'd" around and not liking where you end up. I want you to be able to shine your God-given light and to have a sparkle in your eye that draws people to you. I want you to have a shimmer and an unmistakable glow, and I want you to find your joy and put it to good use in the world.

GETTING ACCURATE

Assessing your current state

CHAPTER 2

YOUR GUT CHECK

A pause to check your engine lights.

You are not alone.

If you feel like you are at the end of your rope at work, you are not alone.

If you look in the mirror and don't recognize or like who you see, you are not alone.

If you find yourself dragging yourself to work, feeling emotionally exhausted and mentally drained, you are not alone.

We are in a collective epidemic of burnout.

*****

As I write this, "quiet quitting" has become the buzzword in the working world news. It describes a steady decline in engagement as we struggle with questions about purpose, burnout, and increasing disenchantment with our working lives. If you are burning out and feel like you can't keep your head above water, I want you to give yourself the grace and space to tackle it head on and the compassion to know it's not just you, it's us.

Burnout is a common term known all too well by the working world. It is defined formally as a "work-related syndrome that often appears as emotional exhaustion, depersonalization and a sense of reduced personal accomplishment."[1] As a term, it was first coined back in 1974 by the psychologist H.J. Freudenberger.[2] It was formally recognized by the World Health Organization in 2019 as "a syndrome resulting from chronic workplace stress that has not been successfully managed." [3]

In a recent study by Deloitte, 77% of workers surveyed said they are burned out [4], *seventy-seven* percent. In addition, in a recent *Harvard Business Review* article, nine out of ten employees said they were willing to trade a percentage of their lifetime earnings for more meaningful work, with the average being 23% of their earnings.[5] To put that in context, the average worker spends 21% of their income on housing.

We are so eager to find that meaning, that sparkle, that purpose in our lives and our work, that we are willing to put our money where our mouth is and spend more on meaning than the roof over our heads. As the HBR states, "The 21st-century list of essentials might be due for an update: "food, clothing, shelter, and meaningful work." [6]

It's not surprising. 91% of people surveyed say that unmanageable stress or frustration impacts the quality of their work, and 83% say burnout negatively impacts their relationships.[7] There is a real and present emotional tax we pay for the right to punch our timecards in jobs that don't fit us or environments that don't inspire us.

Burnout is not just about workload, it's so much more than that. When we are burnt out, it means we have burned through our patience levels for work that doesn't fit us, for managers that don't get us, and for visions that don't inspire us. We are fed up with the lack of control that we feel in our lives and our inability to spend time on things that bring us joy.

As a result, it makes us resentful and bitter, and we begin to feel like we have rocks on our shoulders and a hole in our souls. It is also often the point where your "give a da--" gets busted. You stop caring, you stop trying, and you go on emotional autopilot. You may have moments where you have a short burst of "I'm going to make this work" and your energy makes a short-term surge, but the burn continues. As author Sam Kee once described it, "Burnout is nature's way of telling you you've been going through the motions and your soul has departed."[8] Something has to change.

So how do you know when you are burning out? Here is a checklist to think through for yourself from The Mayo Clinic: [9]

COMMON SIGNS OF BURNOUT

- Do you feel emotionally exhausted? Are you more snippy, cynical, critical, or impatient than you should be? Does it take a lot for you to stay positive and manage your emotions?
- Do you feel stuck? Do you drag yourself to work and have trouble getting started?
- Are you unable to complete tasks on time? Is it hard to concentrate?
- Do you have more mood swings than usual and are experiencing more anger, sadness, or irritability?
- Are you using food, drugs, or alcohol to feel better or simply not feel?
- Do you have physical symptoms such as headaches, fatigue, and insomnia?
- Do you lack interest, motivation, or energy at work? Is it spilling over into your personal life?
- Does your brain feel tired and sluggish? Has your creativity and sense of personal achievement decreased?
- Do you feel numb? Are you indifferent? Have you have stopped trying to influence situations, have your voice heard or contribute?
- Do you have feelings of self-doubt, loneliness, and just general dissatisfaction?

Sadly, as I look back at myself from a few years ago, I would have answered yes to nearly all of those questions, and worst of all, I thought it was normal. I am here to tell you while it is common, it is definitely *not* normal and not how it should be. Yes, we all have seasons of our lives where we may feel some of these symptoms, but if they are persistent for months at a time or steadily build or reoccur, those are all red flags. Burnout, like so many things in life, does not come on suddenly and can be stopped if you catch it early. According to Integris Health, there are five phases of burnout as described below.[10] Knowing them can make you more self-aware of where you may be in the progression and may also help you notice it in others.

PHASES OF BURNOUT

Honeymoon phase

Whenever we start something new, there is an initial burst of satisfaction and productivity in any new endeavor. Energy and optimism are highest in this phase.

Onset of stress phase

Eventually, the newness begins to wear off and the stressors of the situation start to show up. It's not constantly stressful, but it begins to rear its head. You may notice that it is harder for you to stay excited or focused and you may be less productive when completing tasks. You may start to notice physical symptoms of becoming tired and cranky as well.

Chronic stress phase

As Integris Health states, "You will reach a point where the stress becomes more persistent or chronic. As the pressure mounts, the stress will start to show up at work. Examples include feelings of apathy, not completing work on time, being late for work, or procrastinating. Socially, you may withdraw from everyday work-related conversations. In other cases, you may become angry and lash out at coworkers. Sometimes, these feelings follow you home and can affect relationships with friends and family.

Burnout phase

This phase is when you reach your limit and can no longer function as you usually would. Problems at work begin to consume you to the point you obsess over them. At times, you may also feel numb and experience extreme self-doubt. Physical symptoms will become intense, leading to chronic headaches, stomach issues, and gastrointestinal problems. Friends and family members may also notice behavioral changes. A focus on mental health through therapy may be needed at this stage.

Habitual burnout phase

If left untreated, burnout can become a part of your everyday life and eventually lead to anxiety or depression. You can also begin to experience chronic mental and physical fatigue that prevents you from working. Your job status may be put in jeopardy if you continue on this path. It's important to put in an action plan to address the situation." [11]

WHO IS AT RISK

Burnout does not discriminate. We are all at risk for burnout - young or old, rich or poor, early or late career, experienced or inexperienced. Most of us have experienced degrees of burnout in our careers. However, there are specific fields and types of jobs that are at higher statistical risk of burning out. You would expect some of these, but others you wouldn't, so it's good to be aware. According to research conducted by Limeade, here are the top demographic and job type categories at risk of burnout. [12]

Women

At the top of the list across many types of professions. 42% of women say they are burned out and over half of women in leadership positions say they feel burned out consistently. In addition, 68% of working moms of young children feel burned out. Many women feel like they are burning both ends to be great at work and great at home and their physical, emotional and mental health often pay the price.

Mid-Career Workers (i.e., your 40s)

I know this one all too well. I always cringed at the thought of being a cliché. Yet, I found myself squarely in a mid-life crisis and mine just happened to be a career crisis. I was not alone though.

According to a recent *Harvard Business Review* article, life satisfaction is like a U-curve. It begins high in our youth, bottoms out in our 40s, and then recovers as we age. The pattern is consistent across the world, affecting both men and women. In fact, the difference in our level of contentment between how we feel at age 20 and how we feel at age 45 is comparable to the drop in satisfaction associated with being fired or getting a divorce.[13] Ouch.

While the reasons for the mid-career crisis aren't scientifically studied extensively yet, the HBR writer lists reasons I recognize. A few of the culprits: "narrowing of options, the inevitability of regret, and the tyranny of goals and projects completed only to be immediately replaced with more." [14]

Teachers

According to a recent Gallup poll, K-12 teachers report the highest burnout rates of any U.S. profession, with four out of ten stating they feel burned out "always" or "very often" at work. [15]

Low salaries, increasing violence, increasing mental health challenges, risk of illness and national shortages of teachers post-Covid are creating a perfect storm of burnout for teachers. Most teachers teach because they love the children and have a passion and purpose they feel called towards. That passion though can only take them so far.

Healthcare Workers

In May 2022, the United States Surgeon General issued an advisory addressing the country's healthcare worker burnout crisis. Dr. Murthy referenced pre-COVID burnout statistics that showed up to 54% of nurses and physicians and 60% of medical students and residents suffer from burnout.[16]

Those numbers have only increased post-COVID. As Dr. Saundra Dalton-Smith says in her book *Sacred Rest*, healthcare workers suffer from "martyr syndrome."[17] They expect to work excessively long hours on shockingly low amounts of sleep in emotionally charged environments. It's a recipe for high burnout.

Stay-at-Home Moms

In a recent survey by Motherly, stay-at-home moms (SAHM) reported higher levels of burnout than working moms, with 55% of SAHMS citing that they "always" or "frequently" feel burned out. [i] Unfortunately, they are also often the ones that have to yell the loudest to get their "help needed" message across. The perception of SAHMs is that they have more time, less stress, and an "easier" role than working moms, and their cries for help are often brushed off. If you have ever been a mom or know a stay-at-home mom, well, you know that is far from the truth. Motherhood is leadership, and while their team may not have a corporate logo behind it, they are undoubtedly still leaders.

They are firmly at the helm of human beings that need their constant attention and devotion. They are the CEO, taxi driver, chef, nurse, secretary, housecleaner, therapist, chief entertainer, event planner, teacher, and 100 other roles all in one. It is a 24-7 job, and they are always on call. Not to mention the enormous pressure to be "super mom" that so many inflict on themselves. The result is high levels of burnout with symptoms ranging from depression, insomnia, exhaustion, irritability, loneliness, and substance abuse.

Millennials

Millennials are increasingly being dubbed in the media as "the burnout generation." [18] In a recent survey, millennial managers saw the sharpest increase in burnout rates relative to other generations with 42% reporting workplace burnout, stress and exhaustion. [19] The reasons are varied, but many attribute it to growing up in the social media era where expectations for everything ranging from wealth to beauty to inner peace fill their news streams on a constant basis. In fact, one study showed "a 2,505 percent increase between 2006 and 2013 in jobs described with the word "ninja" and an 810 percent increase in "rock star."[20] Rock-star expectations leads to rock-star levels of burnout.

Human Resources Workers

Human resources has always been challenging, but the complexities and pressures of COVID only magnified the pressure. 44% of those in HR suffer from burnout, and much like the shoemaker's children, they are often the last ones to think about themselves and address it.

Startup Workers

Startups are equally thrilling and grueling. The adrenaline is high, the hours are long, the expectations are unforgiving, and the tenure levels are short. There is a mentality in the startup culture that you must work harder and longer than anyone else to survive. Startups have a turn-and-burn level of attrition, and most are only able to stay in it for a few years. 84% of startup workers say they are experiencing burnout.[21]

Fast Food and Retail Workers

This group has come to the forefront during COVID, and the gaps in employment levels have been noticeable. Employees state they are frequently subject to rough treatment by customers and have little control over their schedules.

Often, these positions come with low pay and few benefits, putting retail and fast-food workers at elevated risk for burnout. Unsurprisingly, half of the frontline retail workers surveyed for a recent study said they were planning on quitting their jobs. Of those, 58% attributed their decision to burnout. [22]

Graduate School Students

In a recent survey, 40% of Ph.D. students met the criteria for moderate to severe depression, putting them ahead of their working counterparts (who average 32%).[23] In addition, 35% meet the criteria for suicide risk, highlighting the seriousness of the burnout. Graduate school mentally, physically, and emotionally tests and taxes its attendees, and most graduate students would, unfortunately, say it's just what is expected. As one student states, "There is a common belief you have to suffer for the sake of your Ph.D., if you aren't anxious or suffering from impostor syndrome, then you aren't doing it properly."

Graduate school can be all-consuming and isolating. There are years of 12+ hour days, constant demands, tenuous academic supervisor relationships, and must-meet requirements. There is a non-stop flow of constant grading (that our brains process as judgment), new information to absorb and activate, and often mountains of financial debt that turn up the expectations for performance. This is on top of the fact that students are sometimes also working or have families to balance.

Business Development/Sales

Sales roles may look like a lot of fun, with the high amounts of travel and wining and dining, but it takes a toll. B2B sales professionals in particular find themselves working late nights and frequent weekends to respond to client requests and close that must have deal. Some 70% even work while on vacation.[24] This blurs the line between professional obligations and self-care, contributing to burnout.

Investment Banking and Private Equity

Wall Street is notorious for its reputation for sleepless nights, addicting highs, and astronomical levels of income. Many would say it has an addiction to a culture of overworking and takes pride in its reputation. It all comes at a price, however.

NPR recently featured a story highlighting the problem. A junior analyst described the challenge and claimed to work 20 hours *a day* routinely. He said there was no time to eat, sleep or shower because of the draining nature of the work. *"My body physically hurts all the time, and mentally I'm in a really dark place,"* says the analyst. [25]

*****

The tricky part with burnout is we all know it when we see it and know it when we feel it. It's a different ballgame, though, to be honest with yourself and realize you need to do something about it.

One of the reasons for my burnout is that I had an all-or-nothing mindset. I had branded myself as an achiever, someone that gets things done, and the only shoulder I leaned on was my own. I did not have a framework for how to operate any other way. On top of that, I was in a career that did not fit my personality, and I felt l like I was constantly trying to be something that I wasn't, which was exhausting.

So, let's talk about the major causes of burnout. The reasons can vary based on the person, type of role, and industry. Still, there are common denominators that cut across all and apply to all of us as humans. Understanding the source of your burnout is a key first step in our process of finding and recovering your sparkle so we'll go through the top causes of burnout in more detail.

TOP CAUSES OF BURNOUT

According to the Mayo Clinic and my own experience, here are common top causes of burnout to be aware of. [26]

Difficult bosses or coworkers or lack of social connection can significantly erode your sense of worth and self-confidence. When your relationships at work are not strong, it makes your job ten times harder. Bad bosses and negative environments are major drains to your soul and your sparkle. If you don't feel liked, valued, seen, appreciated, understood or supported, even a job you love can become one you dread.

Constant firefighting, job overload, demanding work tasks, and a continuous flow of unreasonable requests or deadlines are all major offenders. We all know these too well. Well enough that it feels normal. It shouldn't be.

Consistently long hours, heavy travel, commuting, and expectations of working overtime have become all too common. The hustle culture we live in has created expectations of increasingly unreasonable hours. Travel warriors find the grind of constant flights and frequent time away from home quickly takes a heavy physical toll. We feel compelled to give our jobs our best, but giving your best does not mean giving your all. There is a definitive difference.

You. Okay, please don't kick me in the shin and close the book now. Hear me out. Many variables within your daily working environment contribute to burnout. I list many of them above and below. That said, there is a pause we need to take here to talk about you. I'll mention the saying "wherever you go, there you are" a few times in the book starting here. There are legitimate times when you are your own worst enemy.

We'll talk about them more in Chapter 14 in the Sparkle Stealers section. For now, know that we all have healthy and unhealthy patterns that we lug around with us and take from job to job, city to city, and relationship to relationship. Every personality type we'll discuss in Chapter 9 has its strengths and pitfalls. Those pitfalls can very quickly land us squarely in "burnoutville."

Be sure to pay close attention to that section and check your own patterns. Consider those patterns as you are making any big career decisions and ensure that you are eyes wide open about what the root cause of your frustration or burnout might be. It may very well be one of the other external factors we'll talk about, but do yourself a favor and do an inward look first.

Emotionally heavy work environments that require high levels of emotional output over long periods (ex., healthcare, aid workers, social work, etc.). Nurses are especially prone to this. Nurses very often initially loved their job and it gave them a deep sense of satisfaction. As time progressed, as demands increased, as Covid hit and as patient loads increased, nurses increasingly have found themselves completely depleted physically and emotionally.

Dysfunctional work environments and unclear job expectations where the outputs of your hard work can easily be squandered or sucked into an inefficient or broken system or culture. Unclear expectations leave you spinning your wheels or, worse, spending valuable energy and time going in the wrong direction.

Not being seen or understood and feeling the need to prove your value constantly comes at the expense of your sense of self-worth and can be toxic. I once heard a quote that has stuck with me over the years that I think is relevant here – "You are not required to set yourself on fire to keep other people warm." [27] Yeeessss.

Inability (or unwillingness) to take time off and truly disconnect are often self-inflicted wounds. For example, research shows that every time you look at your phone when you are on vacation, your mind will subconsciously process the information for the next 8 hours. It is tempting to check your emails but don't.

Misalignment of your work to your personality, strengths, purpose and skills is the quickest drain on your physical and emotional energy level and the one we will talk about heavily.

Tying your identity or happiness to the results of your job, your income level, or the next promotion is toxic. Hear me on this one. Your worth is *not* measured by your productivity, your income level, your job title, your popularity, or your expertise. I will say that again later in the book because it's that important to hear. Be very careful what you tie your sense of identity to.

Checklist living means you have reduced your happiness to the completion of a checklist. Achieve XYZ goal at work, check; get that next promotion, check; buy that new car, check; take that vacation, check; and the list goes on and on. This is a recipe for disaster and one I know well. Trust me when I say that the checklist *never* ends. Get yourself off this particular treadmill as soon as you can.

Here are a few questions to ask yourself and reflect on:
- How many of these am I experiencing?
- How long have I been experiencing them?
- Which of them can I either influence or control?
- Was I surprised by any of my answers? If so, why?

WORKAHOLISM

There is one in this list above that I want to spend some more time on because I saw it become so prevalent in many discussions with employees in my HR life.

Here is the backdrop. I would often have frustrated employees come and talk to me and share their concerns about their working situation. It typically involved concerns about a boss that wasn't fair, a promotion they didn't get, or a raise that was too low.

I would listen intently to clearly understand their concerns and ensure there were no manager or team-related issues I needed to address. Sometimes, they highlighted a genuine problem. What I found most often though, was there was something about *their* motivations, behaviors, performance, or mindset that was holding them back. Most of them knew this deep down, and it had probably been a pattern for awhile. I often found that many had started to wrap their identity and sense of self-worth around their manager's or peer's feedback, performance ratings, or promotions.

This is a dangerous place to be. It is a big flashing warning sign and will likely impact your physical health and, perhaps, your family life.

Having the financial stress and pressure of being a major contributor to your family's income is one thing. It is a whole other level of stress when you are personally attaching yourself and your sense of worth to your success in your job.

You become so entirely focused on yourself, your goals, your feelings, and your success that you completely forget who and what you are. You completely forget that you are a human working with other humans who need you, who have their own challenges, and who need your sparkle. This dynamic puts you at real risk of becoming addicted to your work, which is a legitimate mental health condition called workaholism.

Healthline describes workaholism this way: "Like any other addiction, work addiction is the inability to stop the behavior. It often stems from a compulsive need to achieve status and success or to escape emotional stress. Work addiction is often driven by job success. And it is common in people described as perfectionists." [28]

The addiction to work gives a high, much like any other addiction. You feel euphoric when you conquer a big goal or have put in long hours. In fact, it's often the activity of work itself that becomes addicting.

In our hustle culture, where hard work and long hours are not only expected but glorified, it becomes increasingly easy to slip into this addiction.

Workaholism is also deceptively sneaky. You may not recognize it in yourself, and your friends will think you are just ambitious. There is a fine line between ambition and addiction. Typically, only those closest to us, like our spouses or children, would see it and be most likely to say something to us about it.

According to Healthline, here are common symptoms of workaholism:

- Putting in long hours at the office, even when not needed.
- Losing sleep to engage in work projects or finish tasks or constantly thinking about work.
- Obsession with work-related success and intense fear of failure.
- Paranoia about work-related performance.
- Disintegrating personal relationships because of work.
- Being more defensive than you should be about your work.
- Using work to avoid or cope with negative emotions.

None of us would start out saying we had a goal early in life to be a workaholic. Yet so many of us find ourselves in some degree of this category for many different reasons.

We find ourselves increasingly addicted to the rush of winning. We feel a thrill in winning against a tough competitor, a challenging goal, or that elusive promotion. We start to associate winning at work with winning in our lives. We may not be in a full-blown workaholic addiction, but we're in the ballpark and left unchecked, it will continue to grow.

It may also be that we find that we are addicted to being wanted and needed. We believe that our performance at work is making life easier or better for our teams, our peers, or the company and that they need us. We like the feeling of being indispensable, and we crave more and more positive reinforcement. The awards we win or the recognition we receive only reinforce that positive feeling. We feel a small shot of euphoria for the most fleeting of seconds and we want it again.

Work also may not be a source of recognition but a source of escape. It gives us a place to forget about the chaos or brokenness of something in our lives. It lets us defer something we don't want to feel, so we cling to it. I know I did that when my dad died; I threw myself headlong into work instead of dealing with my grief.

Finally, that job that drives you crazy but that you just won't quit may have become a crutch. It feels like a cold but cozy financial and emotional safety net. It feels like a place of certainty in a very uncertain world and feels like at least one thing you can have some control over.

The job starts to feel like a warm blanket with holes in it and fraying on the edges, but at least it's ours. The thought of not having that job makes us feel like Linus from the Snoopy™ cartoon when he's waiting for his blanket to come out of the dryer. It makes us feel anxious, insecure, and unsettled. So, we put our heads down and keep punching the clock. All the while, our sparkle keeps taking a daily hit until it's nearly gone.

Some of us may need help admitting we are in any version of this category. In contrast, others may even see it as a badge of honor that we are so "hard-working" or "driven." Either way, being so attached to your job that it overtakes who you are as a person and consumes your thinking and time is not healthy for you in the long term. This may be a moment for you to consider whether you need to redefine your relationship with your work.

*****

This is a good point to pause and do a self-check on your relationship with work. Author Chip Conley, in the book *Emotional Equations*, lists out the following questions to help you assess how healthy or not your relationship with your work is. [29]

- Do you neglect your family, your friends, your health, and other important elements of your life because you get so wrapped up in your work? Is it impossible to put down your phone or not look at your email?

- If you created a pie chart of sources of your self-esteem, how much would come from work?
- At a social gathering, what percentage of your time do you discuss work?
- To what degree do you trust others to be responsible for something your performance is graded on? Do you have a hard time delegating?
- Have you developed a skill in making excuses for why you must work?
- Do you find yourself craving money or professional respect more than anything else?
- Do you lose sleep regularly because your mind is constantly racing about work?
- Does work feel like an escape for you?

Our jobs were never meant to become the center of us, our jobs were never meant to become our entire world, and our jobs were never meant to be the filler of that hole we feel inside. Our jobs are simply meant to be a means to an end. A place for us to use our gifts to contribute to society and, in return, receive financial benefits that allow us to live our lives.

Our sense of self-worth and confidence must come from a higher place, a greater purpose, or a greater sense of meaning. Otherwise, we are continually at the mercy of factors outside our control. It results in constant stress, unshakeable feelings of insecurity, and a relentless pursuit of affirmation from those around us.

It's a dangerous pursuit. Over time, we begin to try and normalize these feelings. We believe they are a normal part of our existence, and we think our minds and bodies can handle it (they can't). We get so used to fear and insecurity visiting us that we pour them a glass of tea and sit on the front porch with them.

I want you to stop fear and insecurity at the mailbox, and I want them to lose your address. Instead, let optimism, contentment, purpose, and generosity come sit and hang out with you; they are much better friends.

****

CHAPTER SUMMARY ACTIVITY

****

REFLECTION QUESTIONS

Reflect through the chapter. On a scale of low, medium, and high, rate yourself on your degree of burnout. Below is a short guide to help your thinking.

- Low to No Burnout – I am in a healthy, productive, and energizing part of my life. I am reading this book more out of curiosity.

- Medium Burnout - I feel some degree of burnout and believe that if I don't address it, it will become increasingly worse.

- High Burnout - I have no doubt I am burned out. I feel it in every fiber of my being.

**My degree of burnout is _____. (High, medium, or low)

**The impact of my score on my family, health and relationships is:

CHAPTER 3

RECALCULATING

Getting accurate on your circumstances.

There is a moment in the movie *The Lion King®* when Mufasa comes to adolescent Simba as he's looking into a puddle of water. Mufasa looks at Simba and says, "It is time. You are more than what you have become." [30]

Read that again. "It is time. You are more than what you have become."

For a children's movie, that was a heavy line of truth that spoke to me powerfully years ago and continues to speak to me now. I have it printed and on my wall.

Whether we feel it yet or not, we all have this feeling deep in our mind that there is more *to* us and more *for* us in this world. The million-dollar question is always, "How do you know when it's time?"

How do you know when it's time to look up from the tyranny of the urgent that dominates your day and take a moment of pause to think about your life and what's next? How do you know when it's time that you put action behind your thoughts and dreams?

How do you know when it's time to make either baby-step changes or giant transformational leaps in where and how you spend your time? How do you know when it's time to make a 180-degree turn or take an entirely new road? How do you know when the time has come that you can no longer physically, emotionally, or mentally continue to be the same person doing the same things?

How do you know when it is time to stop the never-ending mental risk assessment process that keeps running in your mind? I know I often felt like I had Siri's™ wrong turn GPS message stuck on repeat in my head saying recalculating.... recalculating.... recalculating. I am a black belt over-thinker. I knew something needed to change, but I was constantly calculating and recalculating and could not break the loop.

Fortunately, (or unfortunately), for me, it wasn't my initiative or my proactive decision to step into my journey of transformation. Life came along and hit me squarely in the face and knocked me to my physical and emotional knees. While in hindsight, it was exactly what I needed, it was entirely preventable.

There is a much more positive and less painful path you can take to get to this sparkly destination, which is full of energy, joy, and impact. It is the reason for this book. I want to save you the skinned knees and emotional band-aids and help you be your own best friend on this journey.

Let's look at four scenarios, any of which you may be experiencing right now. I affectionately call them the whack, the wall, the dip, and the racetrack. All are clues to whether the time has come for you to start your journey.

THE WHACK

This one isn't so much a clue as it is a cosmic 2x4 across the face. It is a bug hitting the windshield and you are the bug. It is an ambush and a full-on frontal attack that will knock the breath out of you. It is life's preferred method of getting the attention of the hard-charging, deliriously driven, insufferably stubborn, Type A, "red" personalities like mine. It sometimes is the only thing that works because we pride ourselves in our ability to overcome obstacles, punch through walls, and succeed at all costs.

The 'whacks' of life come in all shapes and sizes. It may be the sudden onset of a medical condition you never saw coming. It could be the unexpected death of a loved one. It could be a car accident or a natural disaster that shakes your literal foundation. It could be the sudden loss of your job, a divorce, or any other crisis from life's roulette wheel that we are unfortunate enough to land upon.

Incredibly, for some of us, myself included in this category, one whack may not be enough. Some of us will muster all of our perceived superhuman strength, pick ourselves up, dust ourselves off, and go back to life as we know it, appearing no worse for the wear. Then, in the chess game of life, life will come along, and just steal the king off the board or take all your marbles. It may come a month, a year, or five years later, but make no mistake, it will come.

So, choose to be a quick learner and after you have one whack, pause. And I don't mean pause for a minute, pause for whatever length of time you need to until you feel like you have heard the wisdom of that whack. Pause until you know what it was trying to tell you deep in your soul and have thought through what it should mean for you. That may be a week, a month, or for many people I know, it is six months; just give yourself the space and grace to recalculate. This one is definitely a signal that "it is time" to make a change.

THE WALL

The wall always wins. It may just take us awhile to learn the lesson. The wall is an inevitable and common visitor across the working world, and it can be a precursor to the whack when we try to punch through it.

When I ask others who have started their sparkle journey what was the trigger that finally got to them, 80% say that they hit a wall, most typically in their working life. There was some unexpected moment or 100th repeat of a problem that they could no longer tolerate one more second. There was some conversation they had for the 10th time that just hit them all the wrong way or some activity in their life that was important that they missed yet again. There was some town hall meeting where they heard the same hollow attempts at inspiration from yet the fifth set of leaders they had in five years or some addition to their job description that held no interest or passion for them. There was some wayward comment from a manager or peer that yet again reinforced that they were not in the right environment, and the list continues.

The wall always involves the repeat of something that deep down feels like sandpaper on your soul or bricks hitting against your brain.

We endure it for as long as we can, but there always comes a moment. There always comes a moment when the pain overwhelms our fear, and we feel a new sense of confidence and boldness. Some describe it as something that feels like it just broke inside, but the difference is this was a good break. It was a break of something inside that let the light in, making us stronger when it healed. This one is also an "it is time" signal.

THE RACETRACK

Racetracks are equally mind-numbingly exhausting and gloriously comfortable. It's the same scenery, just a different day, but at least we know what to expect. The racetrack is ultimately a dead end. It will keep you going around and around in circles until you get dizzy and crash. The reality is we are going ninety miles an hour yet getting nowhere, and we are confusing motion with progress. We feel frantic, chaotic, unstructured, and out of control on the track. Our 30-second pit stops are too short, and we can tell our tires are starting to run flat.

This is not a race you can win, and you feel stuck. You work harder and harder, go faster and faster, and as Seth Godin says in *The Dip*, "nothing much changes, it doesn't get a lot better, and it doesn't get a lot worse." [31]

You may not know the end destination, or if you do, it may give you no energy or joy. If this is you, you need to radio your inner crew chief, tell them you are taking an extended pit stop, and then get off the track and onto a highway. This is not the race that was meant for you; you are meant for a different kind of road. It is time to pause and figure out where you are heading.

You need to run your own race on your own track. Give yourself your own get-out-of-jail-free card. You are a highly capable, uniquely gifted, and significant person in this world, and you have options. You always have options. This too, is an "it is time" signal.

THE DIP

The dip is predictable, familiar, and deceiving. It has all the hallmarks of an "it is time" signal, but it very often is instead a "press on" signal.

In Seth's book, *The Dip,* he talks about this dynamic extensively. Every new thing in life, whether it be a new job, a new hobby, a new puppy, or a new company, starts full of fun, possibility, and excitement. Somewhere along the way, it starts to fade. We get into the throes of the new job with all its muck and mire, or the repetitiveness of something that used to be new and exciting, and we start to roll down the hill on the U-shaped curve of life. [32]

Things may start to overwhelm you, they may begin to feel hard, or you may feel overwhelmed. You may experience a setback or something that makes you no longer want to stay on this path. Still, as Seth describes, the winners in life can distinguish between the dip and the racetrack.

I have felt a dip just in writing this book. As excited as I was, about fifty pages in, I started to feel the dip when I knew I had another hundred to go. Portions became challenging to write, but I knew the end result would give me great joy. So, I made minor course corrections, changed my methods and schedules of writing, and got my mojo back.

The dip may be where you need to stay, and it becomes more a matter of perseverance and grit to get through it, if whatever is at the top of the hill lights you up. You may need to change your tactics, not your strategy. This one is *not* an "it is time" signal; this is a "press on" signal.

THE CAUTION LIGHT

There are genuinely times when you should wait to make a major career or life decision. You can make the decision in your head but stop short of taking action until you give yourself more time to think it through. Sometimes, like a good cup of tea, we must steep in our situation and our thoughts to get a good strong outcome.

Here are some scenarios that come to mind of when it may be more of a "give this a minute" signal than an "it is time" or a "press on" signal.

When You are Running *From* Something

Whenever someone would come and talk to me about leaving an organization, I would always ask them, "Are you running *from* something or *to* something?"

If you are in a situation where you feel like you have hit a wall and you feel that it is time with every fiber of your being, great. Follow that instinct but give yourself time to discover what it is you want to do next and what you will go to. You want to walk confidently into your next chapter, not running frantically with the wrong shoes on and your hair on fire.

You want to be in the driver's seat and feel in complete control, making clear-headed decisions and being proactive versus reactive.

When You are Burned Out, Pissed Off or Running on Empty

You may scratch your head a little bit about this one, given all we have discussed, but it is a cousin to the one above. When you are burned out or angry, you are not at your best, and your decisions may be short-sighted. Take time to rest and decompress before you make your decisions. Use the last chapter of this book as a guidepost around what we mean when we say 'rest'; it is much more than just sleep. It's best to restore yourself before you make the decision. Take a short break or an extended vacation; just give yourself time and space.

When You Are Afraid

This is another one that may seem counterintuitive, but as Dr. Saundra Dalton-Smith describes in *Sacred Rest*, "fear can cause you to accept a truth that isn't real. It can lead you down a false path and result in poor choices. When you are afraid, step back and pause. Focus on what you know to be true rather than what you think or imagine and analyze the reality of the present." [33]

******

Breakthrough is just around the corner from all five scenarios above. If you find yourself in any of these, consider it an opportunity or a blessing. Breakthrough comes from courage, curiosity, and choice [34] and all these ingredients are within you. If you can find no other evidence of them, just the fact that you are reading this book shows that they are within you and available and ready for your use. You are armed with knowledge now to recognize it and use it to your advantage.

We will all come to an intersection in our lives. A point where the pain of the present overtakes our fear of the future. In this moment, we know with absolute clarity that staying the same is no longer an option. Yet our fears of change and an uncertain future at times feel paralyzing. Psychologist Abraham Maslow once said that at any given moment, we have two options: "To step forward into growth or to step back into safety." [35] One option is full of abundance, meaning, and possibility but short-term risk. The other leads to scarcity and dwindling comfort and is not as safe in the long run. The choice is yours.

CHAPTER SUMMARY ACTIVITY

****

REFLECTION QUESTIONS

The scenario that best describes my current situation from the list above in the chapter is:

Examples: I have been whacked, I have hit a wall, I am in a dip, I am on a racetrack, or I am at a caution light and need a pause.

CHAPTER REFLECTION NOTES

_____

_____

_____

_____

_____

_____

_____

_____

CHAPTER 4

THE RECIPE

A Framework

No one wants to be in a state of burnout, and no one wants to be a workaholic. We all are searching for a way to make a shift and to find a recipe for joy and sparkle in our lives.

I won't pretend this book will have all the answers for you in your specific situation. What I will share are my hard-won learnings and the insights of the amazing people whom I have worked with for 20 years as an HR practitioner.

The lessons of those I have seen courageously step into their journey to find a new kind of joy waiting for them. There is a consistent secret sauce that, if poured intentionally into your life, can make a meaningful difference in your sparkle.

I think of sparkle and joy like I do my favorite chocolate cake. A set of ingredients make a home run cake every time. There are also a couple of secret ingredients I have discovered over time, based on years of blissful chocolate trial and error (pro tip – 2 tsp of espresso brings out the chocolate flavor like you wouldn't believe!).

As I've spoken to friends, colleagues, and peers, and recalling my own experience, I believe there are four main ingredients to finding and keeping our sparkle. We will talk through these in the rest of the book, but if you are like me and want to know what your shopping list needs to be ahead of time, here is an overview of the process and the key ingredients.

THE STEPS

This journey is a process. It can be exhilarating and terrifying in the same breath, but the ultimate destination is worth every second of the ride. Below is a high-level overview of how to beat burnout and how to create a working life that makes your brain tingle and your heart sparkle.

Step 1: Radical Reflection - Break out your best reflection mood music, take a walk in nature or find the place that gives you the most peace, and dig deep in this step. We just went through the most significant elements of this phase, but this is where you get shockingly honest about your current situation. This is your gut check. This is you getting ahead of the whack and getting ahead of the game. This is where it all starts, and this is where your why comes to life. Get crystal clear on where you are, where you want to be, and, most importantly, why. Everything starts and ends with your why.

Step 2: Extreme Clarity - Clarity is rocket fuel for progress. This is the step where you go deep and uncover what makes you tick, what you value, your personality, superpowers, allergies, and everything in between. In a rare change of pace, you have permission to think about only yourself. Walk up to the balcony of your life and take a bird's eye view of yourself and see yourself from every angle. A big piece of your sparkle puzzle is understanding who you are and how you are wired, with absolute clarity. This brand of certainty will require soul-level honesty and heartfelt courage. Once you bring those friends to the party though, you will be unstoppable. You will develop a sense of clarity about who you are and who you can be in this world, empowering you to make liberating and inspiring choices about your future.

Step 3: Powerful Planning - Plan like your happiness depends on it, because it does. Plan like a general heading into battle because you are heading into a fight. The realities and rhythms of your current life will fight you for every inch of territory at the beginning of your journey, so create a plan, work it, and stick to it. Think about how you'll start, how you'll know you are making progress, and what success looks like. We'll do an activity later in the book to give you a big head start.

Step 4: Concentrated Action - Clear, direct, compelling, and planned action to move you forward one magical step at a time. Progress creates more progress, and the first step is the hardest, but early momentum is critically important. Strike when the iron is hot, and when your why is burning a hole down to the soles of your feet. Make a decision, make a plan, mentally rehearse your moves and make the first step. Then let the sweet taste of momentum propel you further and faster down your path.

Step 5: Crazy Celebration - Party every step of the way. This journey won't always be sunshine and rainbows, but make it fun and keep it moving. Celebrate the small wins, the skinned knees, the giant leaps forward, and everything in between. Do a dance even if you take one step forward and two steps back because you are still learning and you are still progressing. Have an end goal in mind and have something that lights you up with excitement waiting for you at the finish line.

THE INGREDIENTS

"U-TELLIGENCE"

What lights me up may be completely different than what lights you up. Studying yourself like a science project and knowing yourself inside and out is one of the most essential ingredients of the recipe. You need to really understand what makes you tick. You need to understand your personality type, your values, your passions, your superpowers, your allergies, how you define success, and many other things in between.

You need to have a Ph.D. in understanding yourself *as you really are* and not as you believe you should be. You need to understand what about you works and doesn't work. You need to understand how you show up in the world when you are stressed, and where your personal sources of restoration are. You need to know if you have created a five-alarm fire for yourself in your life and if you were the one that lit the match.

We will spend a lot of time on this ingredient, so I want you to be selfish and permit yourself to think about only yourself during this time. Doing this inner work will let your sparkle shine so much more brightly for those around you and in your life. This is a fun yet reflective section, so find a quiet space when you read the chapter.

THE 3 C'S: COURAGE, CLARITY, AND CONFIDENCE

You may do your reflective work and be surprised at the outcome. You may realize that you need to make changes that scare you. You may realize you have a more significant transformation to make that feels overwhelming.

You may have all manner of stories and excuses that pop into your head on why it isn't true or why you can't make that change or transformation. Change is never easy, and it requires intentionality, a strong why, and consistency.

You will need courage to give yourself permission; it is the lifeblood of this process. We too often let the should system of our lives shape our decisions and where and how we spend our time. You need clarity to fuel your convictions and your convictions to turbocharge your courage.

You will need confidence to give yourself permission to take time to reflect and to make a change that may or may not be popular with people in your life. You need to give yourself permission to become something different than what everyone expects, and to take a risk and perhaps even fail.

You will need to give yourself permission to stop hiding from yourself and to stop hiding yourself from the world. In his book *Emotional Equations,* Chip Conley shares that "self-awareness without courage means you know who you are, but the rest of the world doesn't. It is emotional hide and go seek." [36] Your sparkle's fuel source is authenticity and being true to how you were designed in this life.

No matter the outcome of this process, you will be better for it. You will make small and large changes that slowly but surely bring back the sparkle in your eye, either in tiny waves or a roaring tide. It is a win for you and everyone in your life. Reflect for a moment on the inspirational power question, "what would you do if you weren't afraid?" [37]

ACTION and MOMENTUM

Small wins, progress over perfection, baby steps, skinned knees, and stronger convictions are all signs of improvement. Taking one step in the right direction allows you to take another and then another. Before you know it, there is a sense of confidence that you can do this, that your sparkle is returning.

You will slowly but surely feel the gravitational pull of your decisions getting stronger and stronger and your sparkle getting brighter and brighter. Here are a few quotes that keep me inspired to keep pressing on:

"Success is like a snowball... You gotta get it moving, and the more you roll it in the right direction, the greater it gets." – Steve Ferrante

"Momentum solves 80% of your problems." – John C. Maxwell

"Keep moving ahead because action creates momentum, which in turn creates unanticipated opportunities." – Nick Vujicic

Momentum may come in fits and spurts and in leaps forward and falls backward. Failure and stumbling around in the dark are hallmarks of progress and growth. As Theodore Roosevelt once said,

"It is not the critic who counts; not the man who points out how the strong man stumbles, or where the doer of deeds could have done them better. The credit belongs to the man who is actually in the arena, whose face is marred by dust and sweat and blood, who strives valiantly, who errs, who comes short again and again." [38]

Give yourself permission to falter, but more importantly to win.

SYSTEMS and TOOLS

You will need support systems and warning systems to keep your sparkle once you find it. As with any change, there will be critical players in your system that will keep you on the right road. There are two especially important kinds of people you will need on this journey.

One – a champion. This is the person you trust completely and can share your dreams, inspiration, and fears with. This person is a constant source of optimism and confidence for you. They are the ones that will be able to see the sparkle in your eye from a mile away, and they will be the first to know when it is fading. They are the ones that can send you a random note of encouragement when you least expect it or the one that is always available when you need to pick up the phone and talk. This might be a spouse, it might be a best friend, a peer, or it may even need to be a coach that you engage specifically for this purpose.

Two – a truth-teller. This person will be your counterweight. This is the person that in love and service to you, will tell you what you need to hear, will shoot you straight when they see you veering off course, and will help hold you accountable.

They will gently but directly ask you questions intended to help you keep your momentum going. They will be the yin to your yang and may be your opposite personality. This person also could be a spouse or a best friend, but it also could be a coworker or a peer.

The important part is to ask whomever it is to serve in this role for you. You need to give them permission to be your early warning system. You need to give them permission to poke you in the eye and give you feedback when needed.

******

BURNOUT BAND-AIDS®

Before we close this chapter, please note what was *not* on the list but we very often gravitate to in order to feel better (albeit fleetingly). While these may be ok as an appetizer or dessert, they should not be part of your main course plan to beat your burnout. These are, at best, short-term burnout bandages.

Burnout bandages:
- Alcohol
- Sugar
- TV
- "Frenemies" (you know who these are - the people you know you shouldn't hang out with but you still do).
- Other "busy bee" hobbies that are just distractions and don't feed your soul.
- Cigarettes or Pills
- Shopping, Large Purchases, etc.

******

As you go through this journey, you will likely find other ingredients that fit your specific situation that you need to add and others you need to take away. You'll know what you are missing and what you have been relying too much on and be able to create your own unique recipe that fits you and your sparkle.

In the next section, we will dive into a fun topic, your "u-telligence."

CHAPTER REFLECTION NOTES

_____

_____

_____

_____

_____

_____

_____

_____

_____

_____

_____

_____

SECTION III

U-TELLIGENCE

Studying yourself like a science project

CHAPTER 5

YOUR INVENTORY

Taking stock of your career portfolio.

80,000 hours.

80,000 is the number of hours the average worker in America will spend in their lifetimes at work.

If you are curious, that is also 40 years, 9,600 days, and 1,161,600 emails (that is one MILLION emails). Add to those other vital stats based on your job type and it's *a lot.*

For example, as a Chief Human Resources Officer, I also have moved twelve times in 20 years, created 4,000 presentation pages, sat in on over 900 hours of roundtables, and had over 20,000 hours of meetings.

These hours also don't factor in the brain cells you have burned figuring out the solution to the fire of the day or the extra calories taken in from one too many breakroom birthday parties. It doesn't account for the physical effects of too many high-stress, high-frustration days or the number of family events you've missed traveling for that all important meeting or staying late to finish up that must win deal or project.

So go ahead, take a few minutes in the activity below and look at your stats; the numbers will surprise you.

ACTIVITY 1: YOUR STATS

Hours You Have Worked in Your Life: _____
Calculation Tip: Annual Hours Worked Per Year is 1,960 Hours (52 weeks x 40 hours week less 3 weeks of vacation) x # Years Worked

Weekend Days Worked: _____
Calculation Tip: Example – days you traveled for work on the weekend.

Emails Reviewed or Sent: _____
Calculation Tip: The average worker receives 121 emails per day [39] x # days worked

Hours of Meetings Attended: _____
Calculation Tip: Look at your calendar from the past month and do a high-level average of what % of time you were in meetings. Use that in your calculations.

Role Specific Metric: _____
Calculation Tip: Examples: hours coding, hours making spreadsheets, etc.

Other Relevant Metric to Your Life: _____
Calculation Tip: Examples: ballgames missed, frequent flier miles gained, etc.

*****

THE INVESTMENT

Regardless of your numbers, it is fair to say that our jobs demand more than any of us expected. We had no idea when we were bright-eyed and bushy-tailed at the age of 20, with our whole working lives ahead of us, what was in store. We were full of energy, full of optimism, full of excitement, and ready to conquer the working world.

We did not know it then, but we were making a significant investment when we signed our first offer letter and attended our first orientation. We were making a physical, emotional, and mental investment into our lives. We were buying emotional and mental stock in the companies we so eagerly joined. We were not paying with dollars but investing with our time, our health, and our relationships.

As our careers progressed along, only a few of us stopped to think about what the return on our investment would and should be. As a result, we often find ourselves at a career milestone mark, maybe at five years or twenty years, asking ourselves variations of the question. What is this all for? What have I given up? What have I gained? Is it worth it?

THE INVENTORY

I was 43 years old, with 20 years under my belt, and at the height of my career before I started asking those career reflection questions.

I ascended the corporate HR ladder to its highest point and had all my wildest career dreams come true. All the while, I had this increasingly persistent nagging feeling, which eventually became more like a silent scream, that something was wrong.

I had lost myself in the blaze of the corporate world and had forgotten who I was and more importantly, who I could be. I did not recognize the blank face staring back at me. I was not who I used to be. I was not who I wanted to be. And I knew deep down that I was not who I was created to be.

I was impatient, overly punchy, and cynical. I had lost the joyous creative sparkle I once had, was physically burnt out, and my health was paying the price. And if my math was correct, I had already spent 50,000 hours over my 20-year career working, and I wanted to know what it had gotten me.

So, I took an inventory. I took an inventory of my life, my work, my health, my family, my possessions, and my happiness to see what those 50,000 hours had bought me.

I didn't like the answer.

Here is the breakdown:

<u>Here is what I had:</u> Financial Success, Career Success, Lots of "Things"

<u>Here is what I didn't have:</u> Happiness, Peace, Health, Strong Friendships

<u>Here's why:</u> My job always won. Always. It was never even a contest.

Whenever there was a choice to be made between spending time with my family/friends/myself or spending time on something the job needed, the job won. All because I was chasing success and what I thought I wanted. The problem was my definition of success was way off. We'll come back to that in the next chapter, but for now, let's focus on you.

Let's pause here to let you do an inventory of wherever you are today. It doesn't matter if you are 5 days in, 5 years, or 15 years into your career.

ACTIVITY 2: WHAT YOU FEEL

Take a moment to write down all the emotions you can remember feeling in the last one to two weeks. Research shows us that there are over 34,000 combinations of emotions within 27 major categories and that we typically only feel eight consistently.[40]

Those eight emotions are anger, fear, sadness, disgust, surprise, anticipation, trust, and joy. Other common emotions might include stress, frustration, insecurity, loneliness, boredom, happiness, relief, love, excitement, cheerfulness, playfulness, gratefulness, curiosity, capability, boldness, kindness, or enthusiasm.

The range and frequency of the emotions you feel within a given week will give you a good insight into the degree of sparkle you have or do not have.

Write down your list. If your memory is good, remember how many times you felt the various emotions. It may help to look back at your calendar and recall what you were doing during the day to help you remember the emotion you were feeling at the time.

My emotional inventory list:

_____

_____

_____

Now notice the trends. What are the themes and the frequency? How does this compare to a younger, more sparkly version of yourself?

ACTIVITY 3: WHAT YOU HAVE

Use this exercise to think through what you have gained from your career in different categories of life. Feel free to add to it if there is one missing for you. Check all that apply, and feel free to use your own definitions:

- ☐ **Financial Success** (However you define it; for example – you have xx savings).

- ☐ **Role Success** (Examples - you have achieved a title, role, or level of impact that you had targeted earlier in your career).

- ☐ **Career Success** (Examples - your career from the outside looks positive, you are praised and recognized at work, you have promotions you sought, etc.)

- ☐ **Worldly Success** (Examples – you have the 'things' you thought you should have – house, car, etc.)

- ☐ **Spiritual Success** (Example - you feel connected to a higher calling and purpose in your work and life).

- ☐ **Good physical health and energy**

- ☐ **Good mental health and balance**

☐ **Good emotional health and happiness**

☐ **Strong relationships with family and friends**

☐ **Other indicators important to you** (ex., freedom to travel)

Now take a good look at your list. How does it make you feel? Do you like what you have gained relative to what you have given? If not, what would make you feel like the tradeoff was fair? What type of return do you need and want? What level of investment are you willing to make going forward? What is your personal career break-even point?

Every person will have a different answer depending on their values and life circumstances. Every person will have a different definition of success. As I mentioned earlier, my definition was all wrong for me. It did not support who I was or what I valued.

So, let's work on your definition next. Knowing where you are going is the first step in finding and keeping your sparkle.

****

CHAPTER SUMMARY ACTIVITY

****

REFLECTION QUESTIONS

Use your answers from the chapter to fill in the summary sentences below.

*What I Have:

*What I Don't Have:

*The Emotions I Most Frequently Feel Are:

*After looking at my stats and inventory, <u>I do</u> or <u>do not</u> feel I am getting the ROI I want out of the investment in my career.

CHAPTER REFLECTION NOTES

_____

_____

_____

_____

_____

_____

CHAPTER 6

YOUR DEFINITION

Defining the end from the beginning.

Leaving wasn't quitting for me, it was winning.

I left the corporate world 16 months ago. My secret sauce now is less ambition and more meaning.

I had climbed to the top of the corporate ladder in my field, and I didn't like the view. For 20 years, I had been chasing something I thought I wanted. I defined success as:

1 – Job Title and Status

2 – Money

(By the way, these are the exact ones we in HR tell you *not* to focus on or say when you get the "what motivates you" question in an interview. But for me and my personality type, it was the truth).

Let's talk about these two "prizes" because, if we're honest, we are all likely chasing one of these to some degree.

Prize 1: Financial Success

This is the one we think we are solving for when we are 20 years old and our whole life is ahead of us, or at least we think it is. My dad died suddenly of a heart attack when I was in college; he was 53.

He was taken too soon, and I would give everything I have for more time with him now. He worked so hard and never got time to enjoy life, and I'm sure he would have spent his time differently had he known he only had a precious 53 years.

So, I am mad at myself for having fallen for this trap, even though I swore at the age of 21, after he passed, that I wouldn't.

Yes, we all need money, but we overestimate how much we really need. We chase it, and when we get a little, we want a little more. When we get a little more, then we want a lot more.

It doesn't matter what your income level is. You never think you have enough. You think you can never have enough to put in that nest egg or never enough to buy all the things you think can make you happy.

The reality is things are short-term. Things are just...things. We know this intellectually (things can't make you happy), but the message somehow doesn't sink in. We just keep focusing on them, even though they will all end up one day sold to another buyer or donated.

So, time is my currency now. It is the most precious commodity we have, and I guard and spend it as if I'll never get another minute, because one day I won't.

Prize 2: Career Success

This is the one I craved my whole life.

I'm an introvert and grew up in a one-stoplight country town. Despite my best attempts, I'm not funny or witty, was never very popular in school, and I don't have any unique or exciting skills (unless the ability to get the not-so-coveted "super-speeder" designation from the city of Atlanta counts).

What I have always been though is smart and willing to put in the work. So, I thought I would be happy if I worked hard and did well in my career.

So, I did it. I climbed to the top of the ladder and had all my wildest career dreams come true. Great, right? Not so fast.

I had a Mach 5, hair on fire, invigorating, wildly entertaining, and blessed run in the corporate world, and I have no regrets. It has made me who I am today and given me the confidence to pursue my dreams.

I have incredible memories, a network of friends and colleagues I'll cherish forever, and a lifetime supply of branded corporate notebooks. I have memories from around the world from amazing travels and the feeling of satisfaction from climbing many corporate mountains with incredible people, but it was time.

So, what is my new definition of success after all this reflection? To start my thinking, I made a list of things I was no longer ok with feeling or experiencing and I found it incredibly helpful. It helped me create the lists below. As I share these, start thinking about what your answers would be to these powerful reflections.

I Am No Longer Ok That:

- I dread Monday mornings equally as much as packing my suitcase to go home from vacation. It's the worst part of my week.
- Mornings put me into fight or flight response mode. Every day feels like I'm going into battle and I'm waiting for the bomb to go off. I feel a rock-hard pit in my stomach every morning.
- The best years and most precious moments of my life are happening without me.
- The airline flight attendants know me better than my mom does lately.
- My time is controlled by the whims, needs and dreams of other people.

Things That No Longer Interest Me:

- Blazing a trail in the corporate world and leaving a wake behind me.

- Building the next unicorn or conquering a competitor at which some of my friends likely work.

- Creating a bulletproof 3-year strategy that I will have to change in 3 months.

- Doing one more performance review, one more presentation, or taking one more red-eye flight on a plane.

Instead, I Want To:

- Have time to think, breathe, pray, write, and walk up and down the aisles at Hobby Lobby® for an hour. Time to talk to my neighbor without feeling the stress of having a meeting in ten minutes. Time to exercise, dance, travel on a whim, or whatever strikes my fancy.

- I want to work on things I enjoy with people I enjoy. I want to build a business for no other reason than to use the revenues to give generously. I want to generate income so I can hire some of the amazing people I've had the honor to work with over the years, so we can create something that changes the world.

- I want to stop doing things I don't like and start doing things that give me joy, which makes my heart and brain sparkle and that flow naturally like water to me.

In his best-selling book, *Awaken the Giant Within*, Tony Robbins talks about a dynamic he calls the Niagara Syndrome.

"I believe that life is like a river and that most people jump on the river of life, never really deciding where they want to end up. So, in a short period, they get caught up in the current: current events, current fears, and current challenges, and when they come to forks in the river,

they don't consciously decide where they want to go or which is the right direction for them. They merely go with the flow.

They become a part of the mass of people directed by the environment instead of their values. As a result, they feel out of control. They remain in this unconscious state until one day the sound of the raging water awakens them, and they discover that they are five feet from Niagara Falls in a boat with no oars. At that point, it's too late. They are going to take a fall. And it is likely that whatever challenges you have in your life currently could have been avoided by some better decisions upstream." [41]

Take the time to decide where you want your boat to end up; don't simply drift down the river of life and your career. Be intentional about putting yourself into environments and scenarios that give you the best chance of ending up at your target destination.

Also know, that just like I much prefer the peacefulness of sitting on a beach now to screaming at the top of my lungs at an amusement park like I did when I was fifteen, where you want to go in life can change as you grow and mature.

The important part is that you always have an idea about what is important to you, what you value, and what gives you your sparkle in the season of life that you are in right now.

CHAPTER SUMMARY ACTIVITY

****

REFLECTION QUESTIONS

As I did above, list the things in your working life that are no longer interesting to you and list the things you want more time to enjoy.

I Am No Longer Ok That:

I Am No Longer Interested In:

Instead, I Want To:

*My Terms of Success Going Forward Are:

Example: From this moment on, I will gauge success in terms of the degree of freedom and flexibility.

CHAPTER REFLECTION NOTES

_____

_____

_____

_____

_____

_____

CHAPTER 7

YOUR REFLECTIONS

A short but reflective chapter to begin going deeper.

L ife is full of powerful questions. Questions that are so profound, and so at the 50,000-foot altitude, that they hurt our brains if we think about them for too long. They can start to feel equivalent to solving world hunger. Subconsciously, we fear that we can't figure them out or that we won't like the answers. We quickly get overwhelmed, so we return to what we are comfortable and familiar with and never ask ourselves the questions.

Instead, we pack those mind-bending questions away and focus on the fifty-foot questions that we can more easily grasp and answer. We go back to our busy lives, where our default operating systems kick in and tell us where to go and what to do next without even thinking.

We go back to our car lines, emails, dinner planning, vacation planning, piles of laundry, yard work, presentations due the next day, or our never-ending to-do list. We let the rhythms of our lives drive our days, our years and our lives.

We don't ask the questions and we are not intentional or purposeful about how we spend our time, which results in us living a default life. The old saying says, "If you don't know where you are going, any road will get you there," [42] so often becomes true.

Too often, we realize somewhere along the trip that we don't like the road we are on, that our bag of road trip candy bars and potato chips has long been eaten, and we have no idea where the next gas station is. We just keep pressing the pedal, hoping we will eventually get to a destination that makes us happy.

We set the car on cruise control, ignore the check engine lights along the way and wonder why we find ourselves stranded on the side of the road, out of gas, or broken down. Our engine overheats, or our tires go flat, and we wonder how we got there and what to do next.

Our brokenness on the side of the road reminds us of the questions. The questions that have loomed over us in the recesses of our brains and the caverns of our hearts. They usually come up in our quiet or vulnerable moments, when we are weak, or ill, or have gone through something traumatic in our lives. They come up when we can't shake that steadily creeping feeling that something is missing in our lives and that our lives have started to feel shallow and empty.

In those moments, the questions start to flow. Who am I? What was I put on this earth to do? Where am I going? How long do I have on this earth? Is this it? Why am I here? What is my purpose?

These are big questions that deserve thoughtful answers. Humanity has pondered these questions since the beginning of time, so we are not alone in our search. Many books, sermons, poems, prayers, and podcasts have been written and spoken on many of these questions for centuries.

I find the answers to many of these in my faith, and I use them daily to reclaim my sparkle. Before my sparkle journey started, I found that I had gotten into a vicious pattern of wanting, chasing, and getting. I rarely stopped to think about what I was chasing and why. The questions helped me stop my madness and calm the internal chaos I had single-handedly created.

For our purposes, we are going to put a practical lens on these questions to help you in your journey to find or reclaim your sparkle.

REFLECTION QUESTIONS

Below is a list of several different questions designed to spark and stir something within you. Please read the questions, but don't worry about answering them all. Answer the ones that speak to you, move you, and make you feel something in your gut. Those are the ones that are trying to tell you something.

- What is happening in your life that makes you want to read the words in this book? What might those happenings be trying to tell you?

- What big questions have you been avoiding, or what big emotions have you been packing away so you can keep living your comfortable default life?

- Is your foot on the brake or the gas? How long has it been there? When was the last time you stopped for gas?

- Where do you need to go "off script" in your life? What has following "the script" done for you?

- What is your sentence?

Someone once told JFK that a great man is one sentence.[43] For example, maybe Roosevelt's was that he lifted us out of a depression and helped us win a war.

Maybe for you, it's that you raised three kids who were happy and healthy, or maybe you were a meaningful source of good to a specific group of people.

This was a tricky question for me. One, because I didn't like the restriction of just being one sentence, and two, I realized that it needs to be able to change as I mature. The sentence of my very selfish twenties is very different from the sentence of my kinder forties.

There are no wrong answers in this journey. For yourself, use it as a springboard to think about what it is for you right now and what you want it to be for the next five years. If five years feels too overwhelming, pick whatever time window feels right.

- What gets you up in the morning? What keeps you up at night? Are they the same questions? Do the answers give you a sense of purpose and motivation? If so, congratulations! Use them as a north star. If you don't like them, then what will you do about it?

- What is the mark or the stamp that you want to leave behind? This can be a big strategic lifetime kind of stamp or a practical work stamp.

- What truths do you know, deep in your heart, that light you up and give you energy when you think about them?

John Piper once said in his famous sermon *Don't Waste Your Life,* "You don't have to go to a fine school, you don't have to go to any school, but you do have to know a few great, majestic, unchanging, obvious, glorious things and be set on fire by them. That's what makes a life count." [44]

What are your few things?

What are you happy, excited, proud, or grateful about in your life right now?

What are you committed to right now? What about it makes you committed?

****

CHAPTER REFLECTION NOTES

CHAPTER 8

YOUR VALUES and YOUR T-SHIRT

Your t-shirt speaks a thousand words. Know what yours is saying.

My friend Sandy Sullivan from The Alchemy Group once told me that we are all walking around wearing a literal and figurative t-shirt. Sandy is one of the best executive coaches in the business and she is a quick assessor of how accurate our realities vs perceptions are.

She asked me a convicting question once: "Robin, what is it that your t-shirt is saying to people? What and who do you inspire?" [45] She knew from our discussions what I wanted it to be, and this was her gentle yet direct way of getting me to realize what I was projecting was not what I desired.

We all have a brand. We all have an aura about us that precedes us and follows us. We are all walking billboards for something in our lives. What is your t-shirt saying to the world? What do you want it to say?

When I did this exercise years ago, I did some soul-searching and wrote: "I am smart, busy, successful, and please get out of my way."

I remember that hit me in a deep place. Part of me knew it was spot on, and I was probably even a little proud of it. The small-town country girl who didn't think she could get much farther than her one-stoplight town felt like she had made something of herself.

The other side of me didn't like it at all. I needed to figure out what I wanted my t-shirt to say. The problem was I hadn't given it much thought, and I needed a framework or process to help me think about creating a new one. I also had a lot going on at the time, so I just moved on.

So, as I described earlier, that should have been a check engine light for me. I knew I didn't like what I was putting out into the world, but I didn't stop long enough, and my desire wasn't strong enough, to do anything about it.

You may fool yourself, but you will not fool anybody else. What is written on your t-shirt starts from what you value, and it is impossible to fake. What we value in this life is broadcast in living color to those around us every minute of the day. It is broadcast by the things we say, the things we spend our time and money on, the people we choose to spend time with, the work we engage in, and our everyday actions.

Values are funny things. They sound very "Pollyanna" on the surface, but they are extremely powerful. They ultimately guide every decision we make, so it's important to understand and recognize them.

VALUES

Values fall into two categories:

Core Values

These are values that are true to who we are and that guide us at a subconscious level every day. These values are deep within our soul and, whether we like it or not, guide how we act, think, and "show up" in the world every day. We were likely born with these values or had profound experiences that created them.

For example, one of my values is the value of time. I've had this my whole life, and it was reinforced when my dad passed away at such a young age. It means I am highly efficient with my time and always urgent. That's great for getting things done, not so great for situations that require patience, but at least I know it about myself. As a result, I know that anything I do for work has to be high-action or it won't fit me.

Imposed Values

These are sneaky and can work against us in the end. We feel we should have these values based on our culture, how we grew up, and what our family and friends told us we should be like or should want to do.

For example, we *should* be social (even if we are introverted). We *should* want to be a doctor or lawyer (or whatever the family dream is). We *should* be neat and organized (clean your room Amy!). We *should* be adventurous (even though I'd rather stay home and read a book). We should want 2.5 kids, we should be happy, calm, gracious and have it together all the time, we should, we should, we should.

As Sandy once said to me, "stop shoulding all over yourself." Run from the siren of "the should."

Run because if we aren't careful, these imposed values can steer you off course. They can steer you into jobs, careers, schools, friend groups, marriages, neighborhoods, or situations that don't fit you and take away every bit of your sparkle.

You will never be happy or effective in situations coming from this particular set of values. Instead, you need to identify your core values and live your life from them starting tomorrow. Trust me, you will be a completely new and re-energized version of yourself and will thank yourself later.

So, let's do some work now to identify your core values, and we'll also help you call out your imposed values and put them on your no-fly list.

Activity 1: Values Sort

Probably the most important step. You want to spend time on this one and think about your values at this stage of your life. Also, don't worry, these can change over time. You just want to know where you are right now and which ones will likely be with you for the next 2-3 years. Remember that there are no right or wrong answers. There are only *your* answers.

Do This: Do a values sort and narrow down the most important values to you to just 3-5 values. Feel free to add your own to the list if one is missing. There are several different value identification tools online you can search for. If you can't find one, try this one from The Barrett Values Centre - https://www.valuescentre.com/tools-assessments/pva/.

Hint: This exercise is more challenging than it seems. You will see your "should system" come into full view during this exercise. For example, "I can't *not* pick Family as a value (or Health or many other wonderful values).

Keep in mind that you are not saying that item isn't important to you. You are just saying it's not *the* most important thing to you at this moment of your life, and that's ok. The key here is to be fully honest with yourself. No one is looking over your shoulder. Only you will see this, so let it fly.

If you need help thinking about your values, there is a list of other possible values in the Appendix.

List Your Top 3 Core Values Here:

Value 1:

Value 2:

Value 3:

Now, give some thought to those imposed values we talked about. Go back through the list of values and write down any that you feel you *should* have put, but it just didn't feel right. From that list, pick your top two.

List Your Top 2 *Imposed* Values Here:

Value 1:

Value 2:

******

Congratulations, you have just completed an important step. Knowing your values gives you a north star for your road ahead and will enable you to build a plan. It is important that you have a plan to go with your passion and your purpose. As Tony Robbins once said, "If you don't have a plan for your life, somebody else will."

CHAPTER SUMMARY ACTIVITY

******

REFLECTION QUESTIONS

As we end this chapter, here are questions to reflect on:

- Who do you want to be in this life?
- What do you have to start doing to make that person come to life? What do you have to stop doing to free up space for this person to emerge?
- What is holding you back?
- What is your next best step?

Reference Item: Core Values in the Appendix

CHAPTER REFLECTION NOTES

_____

_____

_____

_____

_____

CHAPTER 9

YOUR PERSONALITY

Personality is our engine. Make sure you know how to drive yours.

Personalities are peculiar things. They drive us, inspire us, irritate us, move us, and often seem full of mystery. Personality has been studied for decades, and we can use its discoveries to our advantage. We'll spend this chapter breaking down personality styles so that we take the mystery out and put the power in.

Personality is much like values in that there are personality traits that we are born with that are core to who we are and stay with us constantly. Then there are more neutral traits that are more shaped by our environment and culture around us. It is key for you to understand your traits and your specific dominant personality style. This becomes a significant signpost for finding what you will most love doing in this life.

Science shows us that while we are unique, we also all follow patterns of behavior based on a core set of personality types. While we are not all just one personality type, we generally can be categorized into four main styles.

We'll talk about them below. As we describe these styles, see which ones most resonate with you, and trust your gut reaction. There is also a fun quiz at the end to help you identify what style you are. In addition, we will use universal colors to describe each type, which makes it easier to remember. I became a believer in the power of personality insights and the connection to color many years ago when I attended a leadership training course hosted by Linda and David Belle-Isle at Incolor Insight.[46] Their personality assessment tool is one of the best I've seen and I've used it extensively over the years. Many of the insights below are derived from those early learnings and I use the insights often when I coach employees about careers and their passions.

As I describe each color, think about which one most resonates with you. Note that you also can be more than one color but try to identify the one you feel most drawn to and that feels most dominant. If you aren't sure, go ask someone that is around you regularly, they can probably tell you very quickly.

PERSONALITY #1: RED – THE DRIVER

Overview

Reds can make a coffee cup nervous. They are going all.of.the.time. They have an extremely high sense of urgency; time is their currency, and "done" is their favorite word. They are independent, ambitious, competitive, generally "I" focused, highly practical, highly efficient, hair-trigger responsive, and know how to get things done.

They usually work on a hundred things at once and are not afraid to break some glass for speed. They will dive headlong into conflict because they want to address it and move past it because they feel it slows them down. When I go into their offices or cubicles, I see plaques on the wall with *their* names. Something they won, something they achieved.

They hate chit-chat and always have an agenda. Given they value time so much, if they stop by to say Hi to you, trust me when I say, they have an agenda. They don't want to waste your time or theirs. They need something from you, and the casual chit-chat is just a means to the end.

Title, scope, and compensation are important to reds, and they like to lead large teams. They want work that is tactical, short-term in nature, and goal-oriented. For example, I am an off-the-chart red, and the red in me loves to cut our grass because I can see direct results quickly from riding our lawn mower. (Yes, I know, I'm odd).

They like to have large areas of responsibility and challenging goals to hit that are time bound. They want to solve one problem and move on to the next. Their favorite vacation is something active that keeps them busy. They would hate being forced to sit on a beach. When asked to a dinner party, the first reaction in their head is usually, "I'll go if nothing else comes up or if there is someone there I need to talk to."

Identity Source

Reds often get their sense of worth and identity from success in their career. They are notoriously bad about work/life balance and will respond at all hours of the night and day. To feel confident, they need to be in a position that gives them a level of leadership over the pace of events, and they need to move quickly up the career ladder.

What Others Observe About Them

They will be known as a fast-mover who can get things done and likely known to be smart and confident with a high say/do ratio. If you need something done, give it to a red.

Reds Under Stress

Reds become like fire under stress. They will become snappier than usual, and they will be all business. They will burn through people, relationships, opinions, and things to get out of the situation and solve the problem.

Cautions

In short, reds are drivers, movers, and shakers, highly urgent, and love knocking out a to-do list. They can be hard to keep up with, will leave peers in the dust behind them without ever asking for their opinion, and may not always be the most relationship-oriented person on the team. They must be careful not to alienate those around them and focus solely on their "doing" and not enough on how they are "being."

Careers

You will find reds thrive most in fast-paced environments like the tech industry, start-ups, operations, or any other subset of an industry where the action is happening on the ground. They can be successful in various roles, depending on what other colors they have in their make-up. They are often in leadership roles because of their ability to execute and ambition. That said, they will *not* likely do well in highly regulated or slower-moving environments unless they are working in the part of the organization where speed is valued. They value personal and professional growth and will want clear and quick pathways to advancement.

Their Preferred Method of Making a Change

When reds have a change to make, they want to rip the bandage off. They are either all in or all out. Taking baby steps and long planning lead cycles aren't very appealing to reds. As a result, they will most likely make drastic changes (ex., quitting a job unexpectedly to pursue a new option). I am like this when I try to change and eat healthily. I am either eating like a full-on card-carrying vegetarian or eating hamburgers and candy like a 12-year old. There is very little middle ground, but when I change, I change.

PERSONALITY TYPE 2: YELLOW – THE ENGAGER

Overview

Yellows are your "people people" who get energy from being around others. Together is their favorite word, and relationships are their currency. Yellows seek and crave live interaction with others; Covid was incredibly hard for them. Yellows are highly in tune with the feelings of others and the group. In a team meeting, they are always watching and pulsing to see what others are feeling.

For example, if a new initiative is rolled out, the yellows are the ones pulsing their friends on what they thought of it after the meeting. They are great at thinking through communication plans. If I go into a yellow's workspace, I often see pictures on the wall of teams and groups of people.

There are also two types of yellows – extroverted yellows and introverted yellows. Extroverted yellows are the lively ones who want to close the restaurant down after dinner talking. They are expert networkers. They love party invitations and might seem to be a collector of people in their lives.

Introverted yellows are quieter. They are humble, focused on deep relationships with a core set of people, often involved in community activities, and extremely good at sensing feelings. They are quick to come to the rescue before even being asked and are deeply moved by the situation of others.

Identity Source

Yellows get their sense of worth and confidence from their relationships. They need to feel connected and valued by others to be effective and they crave deep and meaningful relationships.

What Others Observe About Them

Yellows were often voted most popular in school, which continues in their career life. Peers value them for their relationships and willingness to seek out and truly listen to the opinions of others. They are great at influencing opinions and change within an organization.

Yellows Under Stress

Under stress, yellows, especially extroverted yellows, can become like little tornadoes. They start spinning and will call everyone they know to tell them about their situation. It's their turn to call in favors from their many relationships. They want as many people as possible to be in the situation with them and to feel their pain. I always say that's fine, but just don't start spinning at work. It can be detrimental to the team. Find your spin partner outside of work.

Cautions

The cautions for a yellow are related to their ability to address conflict, have productive performance discussions, and drive action when needed. Yellows strongly dislike conflict and can feel that talking about a performance gap to a person or team creates personal tension, and they will often avoid it.

Their Preferred Method of Making a Change

Yellows prefer to do everything in community, including making a change. They will not make a change on their own, and they think deeply about how the change will affect not only them, but the people around them. When yellows need or want to make a change, they discuss the idea with those closest to them, *alot.* They can get even more excited about a change if it's a group effort. For example, if they are trying to lose weight, they may enlist several friends in a friendly weight-loss competition or join a support group to keep them motivated.

Careers

You will often find yellows in highly people-oriented careers like sales, counseling, marketing, service, human resources, recruiting, healthcare, call centers, non-profit work, personal assistants, coaching, or teaching. They can work in various industries but will gravitate to companies with a people-focused product, with a shared sense of purpose and a culture that is playful and values relationships. They thrive in environments where relationships are a currency and where team success is valued over individual performance. They enjoy group-based decision making and environments that create fun and energy in the atmosphere.

In short, yellows are highly collaborative, inclusive, friendly, engaging, loyal, optimistic, and group or community oriented.

PERSONALITY TYPE 3: GREEN – THE ANALYTIC

Overview

Greens are analytics. They are deep thinkers with a keen eye for detail. I always say (and I know because I am one) that greens have a third eye roaming all the time for what is wrong in a situation. They can find five things wrong before they can find one thing right.

They are your devil's advocate and have a solid ability to focus for extended periods. They are constantly scanning and thinking about how something might *not* work. In a team meeting, if you are rolling out a new initiative, they will raise their hands and say, "but what about x and what about y? Have we thought about z?"

Details and facts are a green's currency, and accuracy is their favorite word. There is an old saying that "done is better than perfect." A green would never say that (that's a red's mantra). A green wants it to be right and will only be happy once it is done thoroughly and correctly.

They are comfortable with and respect hierarchy and typically are late adopters of change. That said, they always have an eye on quality and process improvement, particularly when something isn't going according to plan. If I go into their workspace, it is typically highly organized, with certain things in certain places (and they love office supplies and organizational tools!)

Identity Source

Greens base their identity on being right and being trusted. They worry deeply about being asked a question to which they don't know the answer and hate being put on the spot. They want time to think and feel most valued when they are allowed to think deeply about a problem or question and return later with a detailed response.

Greens Under Stress

Under stress, greens are incredibly calm. It's almost as if you want to shake them and say, "How can you be so calm right now?!" It's because they are, as the military says, "working the problem." They are thinking through every step and every angle needed to get themselves out of the situation. If the boat is sinking, they are thinking about what materials they have, what process they will use for the patch, and calculating how long the food rations will last. You want a strong green at the helm in a time of crisis. I am sure many disaster relief agencies have many greens on staff.

Their Preferred Method of Making a Change

On the bell curve of change, greens are solidly bringing up the rear. They usually resist change, especially a change that is forced upon them.

They will only make a change after deep reflection, analysis and study. They will endlessly research the topic and options, debating the pros and cons in their head, and can get caught in a cycle of endless back and forth. They will watch how a change plays out for others and only leap to something new once they are fully convinced it is a good idea. They will take slow, incremental, baby steps and only jump when they are sure what they are jumping to is solid. They will wait for all signs to be green and typically only make a change when they have deemed something broken and no longer meeting their needs.

Cautions

In short, greens are calm, collected, logical, linear, detailed, focused, and deeply analytical. That said, they can also be highly rigid, come across as negative or cynical, and can be hard to build a good relationship with at first. They must be careful that they don't stay in their head so much that they sacrifice time and connection with others. It will make it harder for them to influence others, especially when they would prefer to rely on facts and data to do the talking.

Careers

Greens are typically more introverted and enjoy working more independently in quiet areas where they can focus intensely for extended periods. Greens usually are great with (and enjoy) spreadsheets, details, and data. You will find strong greens often in fields like lean/six sigma, project management, law, accounting, finance, compliance, engineering, manufacturing, banking, technical roles or science. They thrive in environments where they can be independently focused on completing a defined project. They enjoy quiet and structure and are uniquely suited for industries and roles that are highly regulated (ex. banking, insurance, manufacturing, transportation, etc.).

PERSONALITY TYPE 4: BLUE – THE CREATIVE

Overview

In a word, blues are bold. Blues want to change the world in big and small ways. They want to blow things up, transform things, are never satisfied with the status quo, and are always asking why. As kids, they were the "but why mom, why dad" questioners.

They are purpose-driven, and they cannot be stopped when they are excited and driven by a purpose they feel strongly about. Examples of blues in the world would be Steve Jobs and Elon Musk. Big, bold, transformative thinkers who are constantly seeing well into the future and have lofty ideas and big strategies in their heads. Ideas are their currency, and transformation is their favorite word.

Blues are often highly entrepreneurial and enjoy the freedom and flexibility of running their own show. They can be impulsive and will pounce on a new product if they are inspired by it. They are often the determined souls standing in line for hours to get the latest hot Apple™ product. They like to be different, be unique, stand out and are bored quickly. They thumb their noses at tradition and believe everything can, and should, evolve and change over time.

They are change and thrill seekers who love adventure. They are innovators who crave change and excitement and are spontaneous, bold, passionate, and driven.

Identity Source

Blues get their sense of confidence and worth from their ability to change things for the better and from having a sense of purpose. They need to be constantly plugging into new thoughts and ideas to keep their energy level high and to feel like they are adding value to the world.

Blues Under Stress

Under stress, blues are also very calm, but it's because they just don't stress out easily. When they encounter an obstacle in the road, they act like water and will figure out another way around it. They instinctively know that everything will be okay; if they fail, they will fail fast and keep trying. You often hear blues talking about "iterating" and design thinking. They believe that mistakes are just part of the process, that failure is likely, and that they will figure it out. They usually do.

Their Preferred Method of Making a Change

Blues crave change and probably have a Captain Change superhero cape hanging in their closet, ready to bring out on a moment's notice. On the bell curve of change, blues are a mile ahead and out in front. They don't wait for things to change; they drive and initiate change. They will make big, bold, sweeping changes easily and sometimes impulsively. They may not think through all the angles of the change and likely will take others by surprise with their decisions. If they are unhappy or not feeling excited or inspired by their situation, they often will make an abrupt change to something new. For that reason, they can sometimes suffer from "short-timer syndrome" and may frequently leave relationships and work projects early and without warning.

Cautions

In short, Blues are big world changers that thrive on transformation and creativity. They must be careful though that they don't always think they are the smartest person in the room. They may have to attempt to come back down to earth to focus on more tactical topics that others may need their input on or to make a connection with others.

Careers

You will often find blues working in tech companies or roles that allow them to be creative or strategic. For example, strategic planning, IT, engineering, research and development, user experience design, solutions consulting, interior design, art, music, dance, theater, fashion, non-profit work, or an owner of their own business. They thrive in environments that are out-of-the-box, strategic, innovative, and have low amounts of structure or process.

*****

That was fun, right?

So those are the big four. Did you see yourself in them? Could you see others you know in them? In addition, you may be a mix or an even split between two or three of them, which is totally fine.

As the last step, here is a fun way to gauge your colors with the following short quiz.

COLORS QUIZ

Question 1: What type of vacation sounds most appealing to you?

☐ Something quiet, maybe relaxing on the beach or in the mountains with a good book.

☐ Anything with my family and friends, perhaps a cruise or renting a vacation house with others.

☐ Definitely something active where I have lots to do to keep me busy.

☐ Something new, exotic, and off the beaten path.

Question 2: How do you plan your vacation?

☐ I study travel guides and plan out all our activities for each day.

☐ Our friends plan it all out, or we plan it together.

☐ Someone else (ex. spouse, travel agent) takes care of it for me.

☐ No pre-planning. We just figure it out when we get there.

Question 3: How do you react if your flight on the way gets changed?

☐ It stresses me out, I have an agenda, and it throws us off schedule.

☐ We just head to the bar with our friends and start the party early.

☐ Drives me nuts, I'm ready to get there and I pace the airport.

☐ No sweat, I'll just find something to do while we wait.

Question 4: What do you do when you get home at 10 p.m. on Sunday from vacation?

☐ I stay up late and prepare everything for the next day.

☐ Call or text our friends/family to let them know we are home.

☐ Immediately unpack my suitcase.

☐ It depends on my mood. I might go to sleep, watch TV, etc.

Now, count the number of As, Bs, Cs, and Ds you selected.

A – Green answer

B – Yellow answer

C - Red answer

D – Blue answer

See what you had the majority in to give you an additional clue about your style.

CHAPTER SUMMARY ACTIVITY

****

REFLECTION QUESTIONS

In the space below, write down what you feel your dominant colors(s) are. We will use this later.

My dominant color(s) are:

Red – Driver
Green – Analytic
Blue – Creator
Yellow - Engager

Next up, we're going to talk about what your superpowers are. This is a fun one too!

CHAPTER REFLECTION NOTES

_____

_____

_____

_____

_____

_____

_____

CHAPTER 10

YOUR SUPERPOWERS

"No one is you, and that is your superpower." ~Dave Grohl

"Gotta be able to fly like lightning."
"Have to have x-ray vision."
"Needs a big heart."
"A cape and tights!"

Mandy had asked her third-grade class to design a superhero with special powers to protect them and their school. It was a fun activity that they spent nearly the whole day on, including drawing pictures of caped crusaders with big shields and wild-looking hair.

They acted out skits of the heroes swooping in to save them from all manner of threats – everything from hard homework assignments to bad lunch menus and everything in between. She wanted to get their minds racing about the good in all of us and eventually help the students uncover their superpowers.

*****

We all have an extraordinary power or maybe even more than one. We all have a deep down, God-given, fire in our belly, ache in our heart, sparkle in our brain kind of activity that gives us great joy.

Those activities are great clues about our superpowers. Our superpowers fuel our states of flow. Those moments when time stands still, and we are working at our absolute best. In his book *Flow*, Mihaly Csikszentmihalyi has defined flow as an "optimal experience" in which a person feels "strong, alert, in effortless control, unselfconscious, and at the peak of their abilities." [47]

When we engage in activities that put us in a flow state, we are likely using one of our superpowers, and we can feel it. Work is effortless, time is fleeting, and it feels like flowing water. We are in a zone, and we don't want to stop. We lose all track of time and space. We might feel a tingle or just a warm sense that all is right in the world in those moments, but we feel it.

In fact, according to recent research, 15%-20% of people experience this flow state daily. That's outstanding! Still yet, 20% of us never feel it and the other 60% of us feel it just occasionally – with occasionally ranging from monthly to every couple of years.[48] The good news is our fellow human travelers in this crazy life have found it, which means we can too.

Some found it on purpose, and some found it by accident. If you don't look for your own flow, eventually it will find you. You may try to fight it, but fighting it luckily is useless. It's a bit like trying to swim against the current in the Mississippi River. You can fight it and flail your arms, expending your time and precious energy, but it will always win. It's to your advantage to agree with it, swim freely in it and let the current take you to an amazing place full of sparkle and energy.

FLOW

In his book *Emotional Equations,* Chip Conley describes the flow as the delicate dance between challenge and skills, where the sweet spot for flow is about 5-10% above your skill level. [49] I would add to that equation passion to get a complete picture of your flow zone.

In his book, *Flow,* Csikszentmihalyi identifies eight factors that accompany an experience of flow: [50]

1. Clear goals that define success.

2. Direct and immediate feedback that allows you to adjust incrementally.

3. A constant balance between your skill level and the challenge.

4. The ability to concentrate and focus exclusively on the activity through to completion.

5. A feeling of confidence and lack of self-consciousness.

6. Loss of sense of time.

7. A sense of personal control over the situation.

8. The activity has an intrinsic reward.

There is a direct correlation between the percentage of time during the day you feel you are in a flow and the brightness of the sparkle in your eye. Flow makes us feel alive. Flow makes us produce superhuman results using what feels like superhuman powers and skills.

As an HR leader, I often used to have career conversations with employees. I would often ask them to describe their perfect working day. I would ask them if they could create their day from scratch and do anything they wanted, what would they do?

My goal was to get them to start describing their "blue flame." The blue flame is the part of your sparkle where your passion and ability intersect and where you shine the brightest. It is a very cool place to be.

Every time, you could see their eyes light up immediately. It became very apparent when and where they felt their flow. Their voice became animated and energetic, there was a sparkle in their eye and a smile on their face. That gave us a great place to begin talking about what they felt their superpowers were and how that could translate into different kinds of jobs within the company and different career types.

When you use your superpowers and are more consistently in a flow, you are happier, more productive, less stressed, and more fulfilled.

The opposite is also true. As Brené Brown describes in her book, *The Gifts of Imperfection,*

"Squandering our gifts brings distress to our lives. As it turns out, it's not merely benign or too bad if we don't use the gifts we've been given, we pay for it with our emotional and physical well-being, and when we don't use them for cultivating meaningful work, we struggle. We feel disconnected and weighed down by emptiness, frustration, resentment, shame, disappointment, fear, and even grief." [51]

In contrast, when people who have found their calling are living in a state of flow or in their zone, they often describe having a feeling of simultaneous passion and peace. Passion and peace, that has such a nice ring to it, doesn't it?

The challenge, however, isn't just in using our talent. It starts with identifying and owning it.

The superpowers and callings we have in this life often feel like a puppy constantly tugging at the end of our pants. We too often feel it but shake it off. We think we are just average or don't have any special skills or superpowers. That is so far from the truth. As Dave Grohl once said, "no one is you, and that is your superpower."

We all have that thing that no one else does, that one thing that lights us up or that our friends and neighbors come to us and ask us to help with consistently. That thing that if we could do all day, would give us great happiness. We just have to be courageous enough to own it and step into it.

Your power is powerful. Our superpowers can change the trajectory of our careers, make our lives happier, make our teams more successful, and change the world in big and small ways. One of the reasons we often discount our superpowers is because we attach our identity to our job. As a result, we believe the skills we have are just a result of the job.

We begin to identify ourselves as our job. For example, if you are new in the neighborhood and go to a social event, what is the first question you will likely get from someone you meet? It is likely some version of, "So, what do you do?" "Where do you work?" I always cringed at that question for several reasons.

First, saying that I was in HR was always a bit of a buzzkill. It invariably would come with some sarcastic remark or some question about their resume. Second, I knew as soon as I said I was in HR, that in their head, they were "typing me,"' they were creating a personality for me based on what they know of other HR managers. As you know by now, I was very much not a normal HR leader and had a very different personality style.

This is human nature though. We are constantly looking for shortcuts, and asking someone what they do or where they work is a great shortcut. We create an identity for that person in our head, giving us some common ground to build on.

That said, we are so much more than what we do for a living. We are so much more than where we work. We are complex human beings with an incredibly unique set of experiences that nobody else in the world has. We grew up in a certain way in a specific place. We have been to places, seen, and learned about things no one else has.

So, whenever I meet someone, I intentionally do not ask them this question, and instead ask them questions like, "What is exciting for you in your life these days?" "What would be fun for me to know about you?" "What do you think your superpower is?" That one sounds a little cheesy, but it's a fun question that leads to great conversations.

How would you answer that question if I asked you at a dinner party? Where do you even begin to start to find out what your superpower is? Let's go through the exercises below to help you answer those questions.

WHERE TO LOOK FOR CLUES

Your Color(s)

Look at the colors you identified as dominant. Is there a color that just leapt off the page to you? If so, you likely have a high strength or superpower in that particular category. That will at least get you in the ballpark to start your thinking.

Family and Friends

Think about the things your family and friends most often come to you for advice on. Is there something consistent you are known for? Are you known for being an empathetic listener? Are you known for your ability to fix anything that's broken? These are great clues. If you can't think of anything, talk to some friends and family and ask them. Do your best to sit there and let them gush about you. There is a gush-worthy area they probably can think of instantly and would be happy to tell you.

Performance Reviews

Think back on your performance reviews. Are there areas where you consistently were told that you are a rock star? Are there things you are known for at work that people also come to you for help or advice in? Our superpowers often lie in these areas where others have told us we are strong.

Your Accomplishments

Think back through the things you are most proud of. List five to ten accomplishments and then narrow it down to three. Those are also good signposts to where we have strength and to where some of our values lie.

Next, look at the skills and behaviors you used in your achievement, and those could be some of your more extraordinary capabilities. Note that a skill by itself isn't a superpower. Your superpower is the skill that comes so easily to you that the rest of the world wonders how you do it. It is a skill that comes to you so quickly you don't even have to think about how to do it. It's the super skill that is also the one that gives you incredible energy and joy.

Your Feelings

Can you think of a time when you did something and lost all track of time while doing it? When something made your heart full and your brain happy? That thing you couldn't stop doing or couldn't wait to start doing? Can you think of a time when you felt incredibly confident? What brings you joy? What is natural for you? What breaks your heart? What could you talk about all day? What topic could you listen to endless podcasts about?

What and Who You Admire

Who you admire in the world can also be a clue to your unique skills. The people you follow on social media and the content you pay attention to are clues. We often migrate to others we have a kindred spirit with and are inspired by others who may be using their gifts in ways we would like.

Your Childhood

Take a trip down memory lane and think about that bright-eyed, bushy-tailed child and the things you most loved doing. Children are great role models of flow and superpowers. They feel no pressure to be anything other than who they are, and they pursue things that are interesting to them with great abandon. Too often, the world crowds out our childhood passions and interests, so give your 10-year-old self some space in this exercise to give you some insight.

*****

You should have a good idea now of where your superpowers lie and what one specific one for you is. Also, important to note...just because you are great at something does not necessarily mean you love it. If you have one that you are great at, but it doesn't spark a fire for you, then let that one go. On the other hand, if you find one that you love *and* are a rockstar at, then that's the one!

CHAPTER SUMMARY ACTIVITY

****

REFLECTION QUESTIONS

OK, so now you have a good idea about your biggest superpower(s), so go ahead and write that in the area below.

My 1-2 greatest superpowers are:

Next, we'll start talking about the flip side of superpowers: your allergies.

Sound intriguing? It is, so get your allergy medicine ready, and let's head into the next chapter.

CHAPTER REFLECTION NOTES

_____

_____

_____

_____

_____

_____

_____

CHAPTER 11

YOUR ALLERGIES and PATTERNS

The Itchy Sweater Syndrome

I f you live in the southern part of the United States, you will feel my pain. I have a nasty allergy to pollen. If you haven't heard of it, pollen is a bright yellow, thick dust that shows up without fail every spring and covers every inch of our car windshields and trees for weeks.

It gives me a sinus headache and runny nose just thinking about it. I can feel my sinuses ache days before the pollen even shows up. I will, at all costs, do what I can to try and stay away from the crazy stuff and stay indoors more than I'd like. It's the price I pay for living in a nice warm climate, so I'll take it.

Much like physical allergies, many of us also have mental or emotional allergies to certain types of activities, types of people, and behaviors. And when I say allergic, I mean you can physically feel yourself react when you are around this type of work, activity, person, or behavior.

You can feel your blood pressure start to rise and you get the "itchy sweater syndrome." You just want to stop doing it or stop being around it. If it's a work activity, it's one that you likely dread and put off as long as you can, and it's also likely an area you have been told you have a "development need" in.

On the other hand, it can also be an area that you perform perfectly well in, but it drains you. It drains you mentally, physically, and emotionally. You can feel the drain at the end of the day. There is no mistaking the drain and there is no mistaking the dread that comes along with an allergy.

I once led a training session where we were talking about allergies and someone in the group raised their hand to share a major 'a-ha' moment he had. He realized that he was not just allergic, but highly allergic, to spreadsheets and processes. He was a free spirit that thrived in creative, blue ocean environments.

Want to guess what he did for a living and where he worked? He was a Six Sigma leader in a major manufacturing organization! Yikes! Talk about feeling the drain every day!

When I asked him how and why he got into that field, he said it's where his dad worked, and it was a field that his dad thought he should get into so he could have a nice stable career (anyone hear that "should" siren going off?)

You could see a weight lift off this poor soul in our session. There was a light in his eyes and a pep in his step after leaving that wasn't there in the beginning. For years, he just could not put his finger on why he was good at his job but felt so miserable. He was in the wrong career for his personality style and value system but never had the words to describe it.

I know that feeling all too well, and it's why we'll spend so much time helping you deeply reflect on these areas. So, let's help you think about those areas you may be allergic to. You may have a mild or severe allergy, but the key is to be honest with yourself.

We'll spend some time in the end, talking more about your style, but in the interim, as you do the exercise, at least try to identify the areas you like least. Let's go back to some of the earlier personalities we were talking about.

As a disclaimer, about 10% of the population doesn't have an allergy to any specific category of activity or behavior. If that's you, thank your mom and dad, you've inherited some wonderful genes, and life is a little bit easier for you. You can get along with anyone and do pretty much anything if this is you. Still, it may be hard for you to find something you truly are passionate about, and you may even be a perfectionist, so it's not all easy sailing for you either.

ALLERGY CLUES

Reference our earlier chapter and re-read the personality definitions we discussed in each style. Did any of those personality styles trigger a *negative* reaction in your gut? Was there one you knew instantly was *not* you? Was there a job type I listed that you knew you would never like and were thankful you *weren't* in? Those are potential allergy areas for you. Here are other questions to get you thinking about your potential allergies:

Procrastination - Is there a type of work activity you dread, put off, and hold your nose while doing? For example, I am allergic to making presentation pages because I'm terrible at them. It also takes me a ton of time to create a decent pitch, and the red in me gets very itchy about that time loss.

Energy drain - Is there a type of activity or behavior that drains your mental and emotional energy? For me, it is networking events or company dinners. The introvert in me is highly allergic to superficial chit-chat and craves meaningful and deep conversation.

As a result, I usually try to find a corner to hide in at these events. I dread it for days ahead of time and am drained at the end. This is tough for me to say out loud. Imagine if anyone at work knew how much their HR leader dreaded those events. I'm sure it would have been confusing. But this book is all about honesty, and I want you to be honest with yourself. Really try to find those things that take energy away from you.

Performance reviews - Is there an area you have consistently been told throughout your career that you have a "development opportunity" in on your performance reviews? That can be a big clue. Other people can see our allergies much more than we can see our own. I'll pick on myself again. I often was told I needed to make more effort to "include my peers" in my decision-making. The red in me that wanted to move fast and felt like she knew the right answer never liked that feedback. Still, it was clear my allergy to surface-level relationships and my introversion were showing up in my job. I was able to manage it, likely to just a degree that kept me out of trouble, but it was always a struggle.

'Anti-Admiration' - As discussed with your superpower, let's look at the reverse and think about the kinds of people or behavior that repel you. What are the things you see in others that make your blood pressure rise or make you want to stop being around them? Look at the personality styles of your friends and those you choose to hang out with, and then consider the kinds of personalities that are not in your circle. Those are all clues to potential allergy zones for you.

Failures - We all have them, and when we have had mighty failures, we have also had mighty learnings. Think of something you tried valiantly at but failed. Look at the activity and skillsets you used in that effort. It's not the happiest of topics, but this could be an area where you have a potential allergy if you gave it your all and the outcome still wasn't great.

*****

These reflection questions should have given you a good indication of where you may have an allergy. Allergies usually are things you don't have to think about too much. You know them instinctively; it's more a matter of just bringing them to the surface and calling them out.

Knowing and owning your allergies are the keys to successfully navigating them. Once you know you have an allergy, it empowers you to make informed decisions in the future about roles you pursue and how you spend your time.

If you are allergic to a type of work or type of person, you will need to manage your energy and be conscious of how you are showing up in those situations, given you will be quickly drained. It also will help you make smart job choices. For example, understanding my allergy to team projects partly fueled my move to leave the corporate world and start my own company as a solopreneur. I know now this world puts me into a groove and fits me to a tee.

Knowing your allergies gives you compelling input into your purpose and career roadmap. If you know, for example, that you are allergic to detail and process, you will want to steer away from roles that involve that kind of work. Likewise, if you happen to be like my friend from our earlier story, who was in the entirely wrong role, know that you are not alone. It's a common dynamic that you could be in a job that does not fit you and that you may even be allergic to. Knowledge is power, so now that you know, you can steer a different course as you go into the rest of your career and future jobs.

Allergies are one of the biggest culprits in losing our sparkle in our career. If you are in a situation that drains you and you see no light at the end of the tunnel, the sparkle in your eye will quickly dim. You and you alone own your sparkle, and you alone own your career trajectory.

PATTERNS

Remember those pesky patterns I mentioned back in Chapter 2? (The ones I told you not to kick me for mentioning?) Let's talk about them a bit more.

As I mentioned, based on our personality type, we all have healthy and unhealthy patterns we carry with us everywhere we go. Our personality types give us many strengths and superpowers, but they also come with kryptonite sticks.

Here are a few examples of how your personality type can land you in burnout land if you aren't careful.

Ms. High Performer Superhero - If you are a Type A "red" driver personality, you likely have an unquenchable desire for success that creates in you an unsustainable work/life balance (which is really more like work/work). It doesn't matter who you work for or where you go, you are always going to feel compelled to answer your email at all hours and to push your personal envelope until life sits you down and tells you to stop. You don't always have to come in and save the day and you may want to consider if you are trying to go either fast or far, it's hard to do both. As the old saying goes, "If you want to go fast, go alone. If you want to go far, go together." You may need take your foot off the gas sometimes and consider the long-game for your own long-term health and success.

Mr. Perfectionist - If you are a "green" analytical personality, perfection isn't the goal, it's the entry ticket. That's a tough card to have in the game of life. If this is you, not only do you have a third eye roaming and judging everyone around you, it's judging you equally as hard. As a result, you may work incredibly long hours to get whatever you are working on "right." You may never be able to just "let something go," and it can be exhausting to be in constant judgment and perfection mode.

Ms. People Pleaser - Ok, Ms. Yellow, who needs to do *all* the things for *all* your people. I love you, I really do. You need to love yourself just as much right back and cut yourself a break. You are a giver, and you will give yourself completely away until you have become a much more negative and disengaged version of yourself than you want to be. Giving, helping others, and making people happy feeds your soul, but you, in particular, have to put some boundaries in place. Just because you *can* do something, doesn't mean you *should.*

Here are some fun (or you may think not so fun) dares for you to illustrate the point: let a year go by where you don't send out any Christmas cards and instead use that time for yourself. Take next weekend and do just one night out versus two. Take a break for one quarter from just one volunteer committee or group you are a part of, and use that time to reinvest in your well-being.

Mr. Short-Timer - Ok, Mr. Blue, your turn. You love the sizzle and sexy of "new," and you bring the ideas that can change the world. We need you. You need to know, though, that your drive for "new" may be leaving many people and many projects at the altar. You may be a chronic starter and a rare finisher. This may apply to your relationships, jobs, projects, or hobbies. Your insatiable drive and craving for something new may eventually cause you to crash in a ball of fire. In addition, you may, along the way, leave a trail of scorched earth behind you that you may need to come back to one day.

******

Patterns are powerful and hard to change. Knowledge though is also powerful and knowing your patterns and allergies will put you way ahead of the game in finding and keeping your sparkle and keeping yourself out of burnout land.

CHAPTER SUMMARY ACTIVITY

****

REFLECTION QUESTIONS

In the space below, write down any allergies you believe you have after reflecting on these questions.

Here are some sample allergies, but they could be any behavior or activity. These are some of the more common ones I have seen over time.

Sample allergies: social situations, networking and having to schmooze, spreadsheets and details, being pushed on a deadline, not having a structure or a process, situations that are too process and structured, too much pie-in-the-sky strategic thinking or not enough strategic thinking, too much micromanagement and prescriptive instructions, heavy rules-based environments, people that don't value relationships, etc.

My Allergies and Patterns Are:

CHAPTER REFLECTION NOTES

CHAPTER 12

YOUR CURRENCY

What are you trading for in this life?

A philosophy professor stood before his class with some items on the table in front of him. When the class began, he wordlessly picked up a large and empty mayonnaise jar. He filled it with rocks about 2 inches in diameter. He then asked the students if the jar was full. They agreed that it was.

So the professor then picked up a box of pebbles and poured them into the jar. He shook the jar lightly. The pebbles, of course, rolled into the open areas between the rocks. He then asked the students again if the jar was full. They agreed it was. The professor picked up a box of sand and poured it into the jar. Of course, the sand filled up the remaining open areas of the jar.

He then asked once more if the jar was full. The students responded with a unanimous "Yes."

"Now," said the professor, "I want you to recognize that this jar represents your life.

The rocks are the important things – your family, your partner, your health, your children – things that if everything else was lost and only they remained, your life would still be full. The pebbles are the other things that matter – like your job, house, and car. The sand is everything else, the small stuff."

"If you put the sand into the jar first," he continued, "there is no room for the pebbles or the rocks. The same goes for your life. If you spend all your time and energy on the small stuff, you will never have room for the things that are important to you. Pay attention to the things that are critical to your happiness. Play with your children. Take your partner out dancing. There will always be time to go to work, clean the house, give a dinner party, or fix the disposal."

"Take care of the rocks first – the things that really matter. Set your priorities. The rest is just sand."

~Author Unknown [52]

If you are 30 years old and live out an average life expectancy of 76, you have 2,400 weekends left. If you are 40 years old, you have 1,900 weekends. If you are 50 years old, you have 1,350 weekends; if you are 60, you have 800 weekends left. You are running out of weekends; you are running out of time.

If you are a red personality, time is your most valuable currency, and these statistics will fuel you even more to make the most of every single moment you have. If you are a yellow who values people above all, you will think of this in terms of the time you have left to spend with the people you love.

Money is a common denominator currency, but we all have something more valuable to us than money. We all have a currency that is important to us. What we most value and what we consider as currency will directly impact the level of enjoyment we have in our lives. Our currency will fill or deplete our emotional and mental bank accounts, so it's important to know what yours is so you know where to go to refill it. Knowing yours will be vital to understanding a major source of your sparkle.

A Red's Currency

I remember a leader at GE once told me that a leader's most valuable currency is minutes. I was young and didn't entirely understand what he meant at the time, but I understood it very clearly later in my career.

Time was so precious. Time was so fleeting and scarce that I genuinely thought in minutes versus hours or even half hours.

I wanted to make every minute of my day count to give the most value to my organization and still have time for my own life. He was a red personality style like mine, and in hindsight, that comment makes perfect sense to me now. Time was his currency.

For red personalities like mine, if you feel you don't have control over your schedule and time, your sparkle will quickly start to fade. If you feel like you are wasting time or giving it away on activities you don't see a meaningful purpose in, you will get very itchy.

I remember I was once completely overscheduled every minute of the day. My average day consisted of back-to-back meetings every 30 minutes, with rarely a break to even use the restroom, much less to think, breathe, or laugh with a friend. My day started early and ended late, and I needed more time to spend in the areas I most wanted to.

Despite my best attempts to fill my calendar with meetings I wanted to have and to schedule thinking breaks for myself, I often could not pull it off. My emotional bank account was getting low because my free time was literally shrinking by the minute. As a result, I could feel myself physically, mentally, and emotionally burning out.

I ended up sitting down with my team and having an honest conversation about where we spent our time. We gave ourselves collective permission to say no more and to be more intentional and more efficient about when we schedule meetings. My inner red was dancing in the hallway; I could see my calendar freeing up before my eyes.

Managing our time has become especially important for us in our post-COVID world, as video meetings have quickly filled every minute of our working day calendar. Our fatigue with meetings has quickly reached a breaking point, and we all have gone a little red about the use of our time. This is an important currency type for us to manage for ourselves.

A Yellow's Currency

If you are a yellow personality, your currency is relationships. You invest heavily in them and count them as your most prized possessions. If you are feeling drained or feel your sparkle slipping away, it is likely because you feel like you are sacrificing relationships or time with people you love in exchange for something that is not as valuable to you.

You may feel like you don't have enough time for lunch meetings, dinner meetings, or time to connect with your team. You may want more time to connect with your friends, go to your child's ballgame, or have a random conversation with someone you pass in the hall or on the street.

If you are a manager of people and your team or company is not performing well, it will become a taxing time for you. You will need to have more performance-based conversations that you will find draining. Managers with high amounts of yellow often feel like giving feedback is a source of conflict, or worry it will put distance between them and the other person. It will slowly start to affect their usually optimistic and cheerier personality so it's important they fill their bucket in other ways.

If this is you, it will be essential for you to be intentional about scheduling time for yourself to be with the people you value and who give you energy. For example, you may have sacrificed an after-work hobby that you used to do with friends or that kept you engaged with the community. If so, find a way to re-engage to get your need for connection met outside of work. Refill your emotional bank account with the smiles and laughter of your friends and family regularly.

A Blue's Currency

If you are more of a blue personality, who loves new, who loves ideas, and who loves brainstorming, your currency is ideas. If you are in an environment that makes you feel stifled or that your ideas are not appreciated or heard, you will start to feel the drain. If you don't have time to dream, or if you have a big idea and don't feel like you can do anything with it, you will start to feel a pain in your soul.

If your organization is set on doing the same thing the same way, or if it is heavy on regulation and process, it will feel suffocating. You, in particular, will notice your sparkle is fading because blues have a powerful spark that ignites both themselves and others. When it is dimming, it is apparent very early. You live and breathe by your spark and the spark of others.

When you wake up, you want to feel electricity in the air, a sizzle in your thoughts, and a swagger in your step. You want to feel inspired, and you want to be inspiring. You need space and time to think and brainstorm. You need people in your life that you can have thinking sessions with. You need whiteboards, white space, and freedom and flexibility to fill your emotional bank account.

A Green's Currency

Finally, your currency is facts and grounding if you are a green analytical personality. If you find yourself too often feeling like you are flying by the seat of your pants, that you don't have time to fully think through something or analyze a situation, or if you don't feel like you have a plan for your life, you will start to feel the drain.

You are the person that loves the "where do you want to be in five years" question because you *always* have a plan. You also usually have a backup plan. If your world has become very volatile, if it's become full of change, if it's become unpredictable or unmanageable, you will start to fade. If you don't have time to focus, be quiet, or feel like you are in constant firefighting mode and constantly reacting versus having time to think ahead, you will start to fade.

It will be vital for you to find a center of gravity and something that you can control within your life to meet this need. If you can't find that at work, find a project or something you can contribute to outside of work that will allow you to do the thinking, planning, and analysis you crave.

If you have so much on your plate at work that you feel like you can only touch everything lightly, try asking for help from a team member. Consider delegating work to others, or rethink how you schedule your day so that you can spend larger chunks of time in one sitting focused on one topic.

****

Regardless of your personality style, it is important that you understand your currency and take active steps to be intentional about where, when, and how you spend it and where you can go to get more of it. It will be a key source for your sparkle on an ongoing basis.

I once heard a quote that said, "you can't be mad about losing something you didn't fight for." Give yourself permission to be greedy when it comes to your currency. Seek it out, fight for it, store it, and spend it wisely. You and you alone own your sparkle, so protect it and your emotional bank account as closely as you protect your financial bank account.

CHAPTER SUMMARY ACTIVITY

****

REFLECTION QUESTIONS

My Currency in Life Is:
Examples: Money, Time, Freedom, Ideas, Relationships, Facts, etc.

Big Rocks: The Top 2-3 Priorities in My Life Are:

What % of My Time Today Do I Spend on Those Priorities?

What Changes Do I Need to Make to Better Align My Time and My Priorities?

SECTION IV

POWER TOOLS

Practical Tools, Powerful Results

CHAPTER 13

THE DEFINITION & SOURCES OF SPARKLE

Every woman in this world wears a little sparkle, some in their dress and some in their eyes. – Shahla Khan

I once heard it said that "some girls are born with glitter in their veins." That sounds wonderful, but it definitely was not me, so it feels ironic now to write a book about it. I don't know that anyone would describe me as sparkly or glittery. I was the quiet and introverted one who did not like to have much attention drawn to herself and did not think she had any particular skills or sparkle. What I've learned over the years though is that we all have a sparkle, and we all have a shine.

Some of us know what our sparkle is, but we hide it. We hide it because we don't know what to do with it, we hide it because it's so bright that it outshines others, or we hide it because it scares us.

For others of us, it has been a lifelong journey of discovery. We have discovered trails of twinkles and crumbs of contentment at different points in our lives but could never quite put our finger on its source. We get glimpses in fleeting moments, but then life quickly begins knocking at our door again, and we put our daydreams back in the bottle. If we are lucky, however, there have been people in our lives who have seen the sparkle in our eyes and reminded us of it at the right moment, when we needed it most.

They remind us of a moment of brightness they saw in us. They remind us of a time when they saw a spring in our step and an unmistakable joy in our faces because the sparkle isn't just symbolic. It's literal. While we may not be able to see it ourselves, others around us see it loudly and in living color and want to be a part of it. If you want to get a booster shot of positivity, ask people you know when they saw your sparkle. We all have a time when we have seen it in ourselves, in those we care about, or in perfect strangers.

Humans are incredibly adept at seeing, sensing, and feeling emotion through pure physical sight. Just ask the giddy and blushing new bride to describe what she saw in the eyes of her new love when they first met. Just look into the eyes of a dad as he looks at his newborn son or look at the grandmother that sees her grandchildren running up to the front porch to visit.

We see an unmistakable sparkle in our eye in the rarest and finest of moments in this life. We wish we could freeze them, take a mental photograph, or bottle them up. Fortunately, our eyes are trained and highly capable of finding more sparkle and light.

The human eye is an incredible part of creation and is a consummate truth-teller. It cannot lie. They are bare and exposed to the world and are reflections of what our physical body, brain, heart, soul, and mind are feeling.

As a child, I was amazed that my mom could tell how I felt just by looking at me. She would say that my eyes looked tired or like I had a fever, and she could tell all of that by my eyes, and she was always right. It was probably partly mother's intuition, but our eyes are indeed windows to our soul and amazing instruments. The Bible even speaks of them as the "lamp of the body." [53]

Do a quick Internet search on interesting eye facts, and you will be amazed at what you learn about these small but incredibly powerful parts of our anatomy. For example, our eyes are expert light seekers and can detect a candle flame from 1.7 miles away. They can see ten million variations of color and have two million intricately connected parts. Your iris, the colored part of your eye, has 256 unique characteristics; the human fingerprint only has 40.[54] There is a definitive sparkle in your specific eye that no one else has. It's based on your specific DNA, the specific way that you grew up, your specific personality style, your specific set of experiences, and your specific values and passions.

To not find your sparkle, or to keep it hidden, is not just a disservice to you. It's a disservice to everyone in your life. Imagine the world if we all spent most of our week doing that one thing that lights us up. What a difference we could make in the world!

The definition of sparkle has many components. The academic world defines a sparkle as "something that is clear and bright and shines with many very small points of light."[55] From a scientific perspective, most would tell you that the sparkle you see in someone else's eye is the result of them seeing something they like. As a result, their pupils dilate, and their eyes reflect more light. In other moments, a surge of strong emotion may trigger our eyes to create more fluid, and our eyes start to glisten and sparkle.

From an emotional perspective, if you talk to others about if and when they have seen a sparkle, you will likely hear and see descriptions like these below. These are samples of descriptions I have heard and read from others as they describe seeing the twinkle in someone else's eye that commanded their attention.

"It's a sincere and intense emotion. It almost looks like they glow. It is a sign of vitality and enthusiasm."

"It transmits miraculously through the air. Just like you can catch a common cold, you can catch someone's joy."

"It's hard to look away from. There is a surge of adrenalin mixed with happiness, optimism, curiosity, surprise, and joy."

"Seeing someone in their zone is magical. Whether it's seeing someone that works beside you every day in that coveted moment of flow or Michael Jordan on the basketball court, when you see it, you know it. "

SOURCES OF OUR SPARKLE

HAVING THE RIGHT LIST

If you are like me, lists run your life. We have To-Do lists, Don't Do lists, Do Now lists, Do Later lists, Big Dreams lists, Grocery Store lists, and every other kind of list in between.

Personally, I get a weird sense of satisfaction by making a list and then crossing things off. In fact, in moments when I feel like I am entirely unproductive and can't get anything done at work, I'll just start making a list of things I *have* done just so I can see myself cross them through on the page. Great use of time, right?

Of all those lists, I think two important lists can be sources of joy and sparkle for you.

The Joy and Meaning List

For the first list, I'll let our friend Brené Brown talk to us about it. In her book, *The Gifts of Imperfection,* she describes a time that she and her husband sat down to do a practical exercise, which was to create a "joy and meaning list." She explains how they sat down and made a practical list of what made her family work.

She asked questions like, "When things are going really well in our family, what does it look like?" For her, the answers included "sleep, working out, healthy food, cooking, time off, weekends away, going to church, being present with the kids, a sense of control over her money, meaningful work that didn't just consume her, time to piddle, time with family, and time to just hang out." She says these were their ingredients for joy as a family.

Next, they looked at a dream list they had made a few years prior. As she describes it, "everything on this list was an accomplishment or an acquisition, a house with more bedrooms, a trip here, personal salary goals, professional endeavors, and so forth. Everything required that we make more money and spend more money.

When we compared our dream list to our joy and meaning list, we realized that by merely letting go of the list of things we want to accomplish and acquire we would be actually living our dream, not striving to make it happen in the future but living it right now."[56] It required them to be intentional and to make choices that weren't always easy, but they were always worth it.

Take some time here and think about what this list might look like for yourself and your family.

When everything feels good in your life, what is happening around you in those moments? What things are true and present that make these moments feel so right to you? Now check that list against your daily routines, against your to-do list, and to-accomplish list and see how it shapes up.

What changes do you need to make to give you more space for the things you listed? Maybe you have to, as Brené says, "buck the system, take something off your list and take a nap."

Now think about this question in the context of your working life. When everything feels good for you at work, what conditions make that possible? When do you feel a joy and a spark that you'd like to bottle at work? What is true and not true in those scenarios?

The 'To-*BE*' List

The first time I heard my friend Sandy Sullivan talk about this concept, it hit me like a ton of bricks. Until that point, I had lived my entire life by a To-Do list, and if I say so myself, I was good at it. My list started early in high school and continued. "I need to do things that get me into college, I need to do things to get good grades, I need to do things to graduate and get a great corporate job, I need to get a husband, I need to buy a house, and I need to do things to get a promotion."

Being the master of checklists that I was, I was progressively checking these things off my To-Do list, and boy, was I proud of myself. If you don't believe me, check out my LinkedIn™ profile and just look at the successive list of job titles that increased in responsibility every two years. I was on a mission and could not be stopped, or so I thought.

As I described earlier in the book, this To-Do List eventually came to a screeching halt, not by my own choosing. Eventually, life got my attention and made me realize this was an insane life I was trying to create and live; it was not sustainable. Life has a funny way of doing that.

I have learned that what Sandy told me all those years ago is advice I should have taken then. I should have thought a lot more about what I wanted to *be* versus what I wanted to *do* or *have.*

I should have spent time thinking about how I was being and how I was affecting others. How my body language, mood, approachability, energy level, amount of presence (or lack thereof), emotions, tone, and behavior affected both myself and those around me. We are human *beings*. What is it that your inner "human" wants to *be* in this life?

Sandy described an equation that stuck with me. She said, "In life, we so often have it backwards. We start with "Do," which leads us to "Have," which leads us to think how we might one day "Be" and show up in the world. Do - > Have - > Be.

What it *actually* should be though is: *Be* - > Do - > Have.

Your way of being ultimately floods your results in life, positively or negatively. We usually think about our results in terms of "what are we getting from our jobs"' but also asking ourselves, "what am I *becoming* as a result of my job" is also eye-opening. Being intentional about this list and how you want to be, is fuel and a much more enjoyable and sustainable approach to living your life.

Consider what it is you want to be in this life. What you want to be to yourself, to be to others, and be to the world. Let that guide your thinking and doing, and throw the to-do list away (or at least stash it out of sight for a while).

OWNING YOUR TERRITORY

Making choices and tradeoffs in our FOMO (Fear of Missing Out) world and in our "follow the script" world can be gut-wrenching. It's making choices, though, that put us in the driver's seat. Choices = Control. Choices = Ownership. Ownership = Sparkle. We have given ownership of our lives away. We have given it to the goals of our employer, to the needs of our patients, to the demands of our schedules, to the dreams of our families, and to the comfort of our routines. And while we may be managing our territory, we aren't "owning it." Use this book to inspire an owner's mentality in your life. Take control of your life, take ownership of your choices, and be proud of the new life you are creating.

*****

Regardless of where you look for a definition of sparkle, it will always involve a light source. It's often said that our eyes are the gateway to the soul. Elizabeth-Kubler Ross, a pioneering psychiatrist, once said, "People are like stained glass windows. They sparkle and shine when the sun is out, but when the darkness sets in, their true inner beauty is revealed only when there is a light within." [57]

We all are on a quest to find that source of light for ourselves, which drives us as humans. For some of us, it may be spiritual and may come from finding a way to put our spiritual mission to work for the world. For others, it may come from the contagious spark of a creative idea, the euphoria of a new love, or the fun of knowing an exciting secret. It may come from the innocence in the eyes of a child or the amusement of an exciting new adventure. It may come from the thrill of conquering an impossible goal or the contentment of an authentically lived life.

Tactically, we might find it in a company we love, a friendship that completes us, a job that fits us, a volunteer role that fills us, or a new dream that inspires us. Regardless of where you find it, you nevertheless must find it. It will be impossible to ignore when you find it, but you can have moments and seasons where you feel like you have lost it. Your whole body, heart, and mind will ache to find it, so it's important to know where you may have lost it.

CHAPTER SUMMARY ACTIVITY

****

REFLECTION QUESTIONS

Joy and Meaning List

Reflect on these questions:

- When everything feels good for you at work, what conditions make that possible?
- What is true and not true in those scenarios?
- When do you feel joy and a spark you would like to bottle at work?

List out 3-4 things that are true when you feel the most joy and meaning at work.

Contribution List

- What are two to three things you most want to contribute to the world, your community, your workplace, or any other audience you feel drawn towards?
- What do you want to see more of in the world?
- What are you uniquely gifted with to bring?

Fill in the blanks for yourself below.

In this life, I want to bring _____ and _____ to _____.

Example: In this life, I want to bring kindness and clarity to the working world.

To-*BE* List

Now, based on what you want to *bring* to the world, think about how you must *be* in the world.

To bring _____ and _____ to _____, I must be _____, _____, and _____.

Example: To bring kindness and clarity to the working world, I must be bold, authentic, and clear.

CHAPTER REFLECTION NOTES

_____

_____

_____

_____

_____

_____

_____

_____

_____

CHAPTER 14

SPARKLE STEALERS

Be on your guard.

I first felt a sparkle when I was 25.

I had joined General Electric, a company I loved, and it fit me like a glove. I was surrounded by incredibly smart, humble, funny, and caring people. I was in a groove, getting broader and broader roles and enjoying every minute.

In fact, I remember one of my clients saying that I was so energetic and enamored with the company that he could still see the pixie dust they sprinkled on me during orientation. It was a bit of a dig because he probably was telling me I was a little too "rosy-colored glasses" about the company. Still, he was right, and while he didn't know it, he was indirectly showing me that I had a sparkle that others could see.

I was too young and naive to know how rare that feeling was and that it was not easily replaceable. As I mentioned earlier, I later ended up sacrificing my sparkle to chase other things that I thought I wanted. As a result, I ended up setting myself on a trajectory that would slowly but surely take every bit of sparkle I had out of my eye.

I've learned the hard way about the things that can steal your sparkle, so I want to save you the heartache. Below are some of the land mines, big rocks and traps you can fall into if you are not careful.

These are from my experience, talking to many others, and hearing their experiences. Remarkably, they are all consistent, which is good news because it means that we can easily know them and more readily avoid them.

Our sparkle doesn't disappear overnight. It is most usually a slow fade. Catching the fade early can be vital in saving it.

THIEF 1: THE SHOE THAT DOESN'T FIT

Stephen was a successful executive who had enjoyed a great history of joining companies and making a meaningful impact. So, he was excited when he accepted an offer with another new and exciting company and was eager to jump in and make an immediate impact. He loved the thrill of change.

This company, however, had become notorious internally for its culture of what they called "organ rejection." On the outside, it appeared to be a great culture with incredible areas of impact and positivity.

However, every new leader hired into the company was warned that organ rejection was a real risk. Veteran employees told them to be sensitive about how they were or were not fitting into the company.

As it turned out, the company was challenged with being open to different working styles and personalities (this is a more common challenge for companies than you might think). This company had a culture as strong as steel that flexed very little. As a result, it was apparent quickly whether someone fit the traditional mold or not.

As a result, turnover was high for leaders that came in from the outside. Despite Stephen's best intentions, even he became part of the statistic as he resigned soon after joining. As Stephen later described it, for him, this was a pivotal moment. His confidence level had been significantly affected given this was the first time he felt like he had been unsuccessful in a role.

The experience impacted him so much that he began to question everything from his skills to his choice of career path. Luckily, he had strong mentors who gave him good advice and reminded him of his impact and the joy in his eyes when he did this work. As a result, he went on to have a successful career, but he nearly left a career that gave him tremendous joy based on his experience with that one company.

Whenever you join a new company, there are three things you should look at very closely before popping the bubbly and signing your offer letter. These things will help you ensure you are setting yourself up for success right from the start.

Three Things to Pay Attention To

1. Channel your inner teacher's pet and do your homework.

Find out what makes the company *really* tick. Listen for what they aren't saying as much as what they are saying. Research them like an investigative journalist. Look at their website for clues about their culture, or read Glassdoor™ reviews (albeit with a grain of salt).

Check LinkedIn™ and see if you can find other people that work there and talk to them, read their annual report, and check their social media feeds. When you join a new company, it is in many ways equivalent to getting married and the annual Thanksgiving dinner.

The difference is every day is like Thanksgiving at your new company, with its expectations for passing the plate, laughing at the jokes, and fitting in. If you don't like the people around the dinner table, if you don't like how they make their gravy, and if they don't laugh at your jokes, you'll lose your work sparkle fast. 365 days of Thanksgiving a year is hard to stomach and fake your way through (and terrible for your emotional waistline).

There is a saying that says, "culture eats strategy for breakfast." It also eats mismatched personalities for lunch. Despite many well-intended DE&I initiatives (Diversity, Equity, and Inclusion), culture is hard to change. You'll know quickly what the culture and vibe are. If you do fit in, you'll have a pep in your step and energy in your soul because you feel like you belong. Belonging is one of our deepest cravings as humans. If you don't fit, it will feel like you're wearing an itchy sweater all day, and you want to get it off.

It will feel lonely and difficult and like you are walking uphill in the snow barefoot half the time. Do your homework and trust your gut as you go through the interview process. This one is a major offender on the sparkle stealer list.

2. Make sure the pants still fit. Do a gut check that the job type still fits your personality and values.

Even if you have been in a specific job for years and are good at it, if it doesn't feel like it fits you anymore, pay attention to your gut. For new positions, look at the job posting and pay attention to the first few bullets under the description because those describe most of the job. Think about what you will be doing day in and day out. Is it is going to give you energy or is going to drain you? What parts of the job will you look forward to? What portions of the job will you dread? What's the ratio?

So many people get stuck in careers that don't fit them for lots of well-intended reasons. For example, they went to college and earned a degree in law because they thought that's what they wanted to do (or because that's what their family wanted them to do). Then, five years later, they figure out they are pretty miserable in that job.

Maybe times were tough, and it was hard to find a job when you were starting. So, you took what you could and got deeper and deeper into it. Now you feel like you have invested too much time to go a different direction. Or it could be that you don't want to disappoint someone or put your financial situation at risk.

Or maybe someone came and tapped you on the shoulder for a new job or promotion, and you felt like you couldn't turn it down. We see this dynamic often in frontline managers.

According to research, 70% of frontline managers said they were surprised to receive the promotion they received to people leader. Seventeen percent only took the role because it seemed like the right next step, and an additional 19% took it for the pay raise.

Unfortunately, 18% of leaders regret taking the role, and another 41% doubt whether it was the right move.[58] 40% of managers took the job initially for the wrong reasons and ended up getting 'bumper car'd into a career path that may not have been the best for them. Someone nudged them and steered them in a different direction.

Learning: A key factor in keeping your sparkle is owning your career and being intentional and thoughtful about roles you take.

3. Bring your matchmaking skills to the party and make sure your prospective manager is a match for you.

The adage that people don't leave companies; they leave managers, is very true. I know we've all got a story of a manager that literally drove us up the wall and out the door. I know I do.

Research shows that 57% of employees have left a job because of their manager. Fourteen percent have left multiple positions because of their managers, and an additional 32% have seriously considered quitting because of their manager.[59] Spend as much time as you can with that hiring manager. Consider asking if you could do a lunch interview to be in a more casual setting to get to know them better.

Look at their LinkedIn™ profile. It is a gold mine of information. Take what you have learned here about personality styles and colors and do some detective work on what their colors might be. The words they use in their profile scream their personality type and color, and it's pretty easy to figure someone out based on what they put on social media. Think about how their personality type will gel with yours. Consider the success, or not, that you have had working with that kind of personality in the past.

Also, as much as you may do your homework on one specific manager, be prepared to have multiple managers in a shorter timeframe than you would like.

I once joined a company where it was normal for someone to have three or four managers in a year. Change and reorganization were constant as the company tried to find its footing. This is especially common in high-growth industries like technology or startups.

It is also common in large, highly matrixed organizations that you may have more than one manager at one time. You'll have a direct manager and a dotted line manager. I had that dynamic often, which meant I had to learn quickly to understand both expectations and personality styles.

If you prefer to avoid change, be cautious if you are considering joining companies where the pace of change is above the norm or where there are heavily matrix organizational structures. You may be able to navigate it, but it will ultimately take a heavy emotional and mental toll on you.

This category of sparkle stealers - work type and environment- considerably influences your sparkle at work.

Invest as much time as possible to research these three areas when joining a new company. If you are not in the job market, audit your current environment and think about how it shakes out in this analysis.

The homework you do in this category is well worth the time investment and could save you considerable frustration down the road. In the Appendix, we have included a link to bonus material that you can use to audit your current environment.

THIEF 2: SIDE EYEING AND NAVEL GAZING

Comparison is a thief. It is a master at its craft and one of the fastest ways to extinguish your sparkle.

Doing the side eye - looking to your left and right to see what your colleagues are doing and getting in their careers- will quickly darken your soul and dim the light in your eye.

You will begin to have all the questions in your head around why them and not you, and it will trigger nothing but an avalanche of insecurity and jealousy. I have seen even the best performers and the highest potential employees fall into this trap.

As an HR leader, I cannot tell you the number of conversations and the number of hours I have spent listening to a disgruntled employee talk about this dynamic. They talk about being passed over for a promotion, how it wasn't fair, and that there must be some nefarious reason for it. I can see it on their face when they walk in the door. I can see the frustration, confusion, and anger a mile away. I can see the navel-gazing that I know will ultimately be a career derailer for them if they don't get past it.

They are sitting in judgment of their manager and peers. They are thinking out of a mentality of scarcity vs. abundance. A verse in the Bible comes to mind whenever I think about this topic, which says, "Why do you look at the speck of sawdust in your brother's eye and pay no attention to the plank in your own eye?" [60]

I can tell you that 90% of the time I had a conversation with someone like this, they had a 10-foot-long plank in their eye that they were not addressing. Something about their performance or their way of performing (we called it 'the what' and 'the how' equation in HR) was holding them back. And they didn't want to see or didn't want to admit it.

In those conversations, I always tried to have the person lift their eyes and see the bigger picture. I wanted them to see the bigger picture of the team, the company, and, most importantly, their own bigger picture. I wanted them to get on the balcony and look down and see what was working and was not working about them. I wanted them to see their unique gifts and skills and consider if they were in a position to use them. If they weren't, we would talk about what was holding them back that was in their control to influence.

I wanted them to think about when they had a sparkle, when they lost it and why. I wanted them to reclaim a sense of purpose that would enable them to shine so brightly in their job that their manager would never be able to ignore it.

THIEF 3: SCARCITY MINDSET

Have you ever paid attention to what you are thinking? Have you ever stopped to think about the pattern of the tone of your thoughts? Are they negative more than positive? Are they cynical versus optimistic? Do you feel like the world is out to get you? Do you think there is not enough in the world to go around?

Do you focus on what could happen or what might be around the corner versus what is happening now and is right in front of you? Do you focus more on what you *don't* have versus what you do have? Do you have dreams but feel like you don't have the right means or resources to achieve them, or do you instead see people that might be willing to help you?

Depending on your answers, you may be seeing the world through a lens of scarcity or a lens of abundance. I've mentioned this concept a couple of times and some of you may have heard of it before. If you haven't, I want to spend a few minutes on them. They are essential components of how we see the world and are directly tied to our level of happiness, joy, and sparkle.

One of my favorite quotes is, "The mind is everything. What you think, you become." [61] Science has proven that our mindset has a direct impact on the longevity of our life. For example, researchers at Yale and Miami revealed that those with more positive beliefs around aging lived 7.5 years longer than those with less positive self-perceptions of aging. Incredibly, that is more of a positive impact than lowering your blood pressure, stopping smoking and regular exercise can give you. [62] The mind is a wonderfully powerful tool.

Over 25 years ago, author Steven Covey introduced the concepts of abundance and scarcity in our thinking patterns.[63] An abundance mindset believes there is more than enough of everything in the world to go around. There is enough money, enough love, enough options, opportunity, knowledge, food, available promotions, and toilet paper for everyone. It flows from a core sense of self-worth, love for yourself and others, and of contentment.

It gives you a sense of peace and security when everything around you turns into chaos. It gives you a sense of confidence that everything will be okay that will seem unusual to others. It gives you a sparkle that attracts others. It makes you more resilient and more successful over the long term because it gives you a sense that everything is possible.

Abundance mindsets see possibility. It empowers you and those around you. It is optimistic, brave, bold, generous, and kind. It is loving, it is trusting, it is patient, and collaborative, and it does not compare itself to others. In a negotiation, it doesn't see winning and losing. It sees options for winning for all sides by expanding the possibilities and making the pie bigger.

A scarcity mindset, on the other hand, is the more common of the two and is fueled by the culture of the world, the daily news, and even the way we have designed our working world. This pervasive mindset believes that there will never be enough in the world to go around and that you are constantly competing with your neighbor.

We saw this dynamic up close and personal during the COVID pandemic. The mad scramble to buy every scrap of toilet paper, every bottle of hand sanitizer and every last box of macaroni was fueled by this mentality. Even though there was more than enough to go around, our scarcity thinking propelled us to believe that we had to go into protection mode for ourselves, at the expense of our neighbor.

As a result, we saw extreme shortages of daily necessities, and we created our own scarcity monster with our own hands and our own credit cards.

I once read a fun example of this contrasting dynamic. There is a story about a company that manufactures and sells shoes that sent out two marketing scouts to a brand-new market they had never been to. The first scout relayed back a message that said, "Situation hopeless. Stop, no one wears shoes."

The second scout also sent back a message but said, "Glorious business opportunity. Stop everything and send goods immediately; they have no shoes to wear." [64] What a difference!

In our day-to-day working world, if we think like the first scout, it means we believe we are in constant competition with our peers. It makes us feel that we need to hoard our knowledge to have more power or that we have to hoard our supply of sticky notes because we won't ever get any more.

It means you believe your coworker's gain, promotion, salary increase, or fancy new desk chair is your loss. You think they got something that there was only one of, and now you will never be able to get it. It means that when you think about making a career change, you will throw up all kinds of imagined obstacles. For example, you might say no one is hiring, you don't have the right skills or connections, or the competition will be too strong.

So, our fears, scarcity thinking, and insecurities stop us in our tracks, and like thieves in the night, steal our sparkle. You cannot sparkle when you are hiding behind a defensive shield, hiding behind a mask, or sitting in the corner counting all of your toilet paper. The world we live in paves the way for this kind of thinking, which can grow like cancer. It will stop you from living your best life right now because you are too worried about fortifying yourself for a scary and unknown future.

It will keep you constantly looking over your shoulder and out the side of your eye at your neighbor or peer. It will keep your fist clenched tight instead of flat, open, and ready to receive the gifts the world may have for you. It will keep your circle of friends small and your sphere of influence smaller. It will keep you fearful, anxious, cynical, pessimistic, frustrated, disappointed, angry, and powerless.

Living your life out of this mindset may give you short-term wins on life's battlefield, but you still lose. For example, you may feel vindicated when you are safe and sound in your position of comfort with your 45 rolls of toilet paper, especially when you see others struggle because you think they didn't plan as well as you did. You have a sense of "see, I told you so, see the world is going to pot just like I said it would, see I told you that manager was out to get me."

Whatever you are looking for in this life, you can find. If you are looking for evidence to support your way of thinking, there are likely more than enough examples for you to prove your case one way or the other. This will be true on both sides of the fence.

If you are looking for evidence of scarcity, you will find it. It is the blessing, and the curse of our modern lives, where information and opinions are overflowing but wisdom is in short supply.

There is an old Native American story that I always think about when I think about this topic. It goes like this:

> *"Once upon a time, a young Native American boy received a beautiful drum as a gift and took it outside to play. When his friend saw it, he asked if he could play with it, but the boy felt torn. He didn't want to share his new present, so he angrily cried, "No!"*
>
> *In his guilt, his friend ran away crying, and the boy went to his grandfather for advice. The elder listened quietly and then replied. 'I often feel as though two wolves are fighting inside me.*
>
> *One is greedy and full of arrogance and pride, but the other is peaceful and generous. They are always struggling, and you, my boy, have those same two wolves inside of you.'*
>
> *Which one will win? asked the boy.*
>
> *The elder smiled and said, "The one you feed."* [65]

We control our happiness. What you feed your mind and soul with is powerful. It can be a source of positivity, abundance, and sparkle, or fear, negativity, and powerlessness.

Given a choice between the two, I choose the former. Despite my wiring that so easily allows me to find everything wrong with a situation or everything bad in the world, I consciously force myself to think out of abundance, to see the good in others and the good in the world. It has made a significant difference in my life and in finding my sparkle again.

Give yourself space and time to think about this for yourself. Ask someone that knows you well which one they think you live out of. You probably already know the answer, but it can be enlightening to see how others describe it and the impact it may have on them.

THIEF 4: RUT STORIES

We all have them. We all have stories we tell ourselves that give us great inspiration or enable us to be our worst enemy. Buddha once said, "What you think, you become. What you feel, you attract. What you imagine, you create." [66]

I believe that is true. Our stories shape, expand, limit, or define us. For many of us, we tend to get stuck in "rut" stories. Stories that keep us from our greatest potential, keep us from taking a chance and often keep us from finding our sparkle.

In Robert Hargrove's book, *Masterful Coaching*, he talks about various kinds of rut stories. [67] Read these below and see if any of these apply to you.

The "I Have No Choice" Story

"I *have* to go to that 3-day offsite." "I *have* to respond to my boss' email, even if it's after hours." "I *have* to be in the office every day to be seen." "I *have* to fly to Dallas to meet that customer." "I have to take that extra shift, they need me." I have *no* choice.

This rut story had me by the back of the neck for years. Just look at my frequent flier levels and the bags under my eyes as proof. I thought there was no way I could not do those things. I had no role models or framework that told me I had a choice, and I was a senior executive in HR. Yes, we would always say the party line that we valued work-life balance, but I never truly felt I had a choice. It's why the job always won.

If you need evidence that you can choose how your working life is designed, look no further than April 2020 and the Covid pandemic. Every company and every executive that swore they could never work remotely and that the model would never work was wrong. Where there is a strong enough will, there is always a way. Life is a series of choices that you control. Yes, if you don't respond to your boss with lightning speed, then maybe you don't get that promotion. But maybe you do. And even if you don't get it, what you *do* get is your sanity and a life.

The result of this story: Someone else is driving your life, your minutes, your hours and your days. Choices and tradeoffs are everywhere, just make sure *you* are the one driving.

The "I Need Other People's Approval" Story

This is the desire for approval and the fear of rejection that consumes our thinking and can keep us frozen in place. This is becoming more common and apparent in our social media-driven world, where likes and loves begin to underpin our sense of worth.

The result: We focus more on appearance than progress and we freeze in place. We live out an artificial and inauthentic life that steals our soul.

The "Victim" Story

This is when someone attributes their perceived negative situation to be the fault of everyone else around them. Whenever I am around someone like this, I often think of the old saying, "wherever you go, there you are." If this is you – if you feel like you are always looking left and right instead of in the mirror when something happens, you may be in this rut.

The result: You give away your power. You forfeit all your power to other people or the situation, and then lose the ability to create what you want. It also pushes people that could help you away from you.

The "I'm Afraid to Lose What I Have" Story

This one is big for the green personality who is risk averse. It is told by people who put off their visions, dreams, and aspirations to keep their security. They "complain about their lives not being satisfying but create lots of reasons for standing still." [68]

The result: Spending a whole lifetime getting ready for everything to fall into place only to realize that, "like sour milk, they are past their expiration date." [69] Life and opportunities pass you by.

The "Why Bother?" Story

People who tell this sad story say they cannot create what they want because their possibilities and choices are limited: "I don't have time," "I can't make that decision," "It's not in the budget." Often, the story is a cover-up for them wanting to stay in their comfort zone or for not wanting to take responsibility. There is often an underlying attitude of resignation.

The result: You get stuck in this story and lose the ability to see the possibilities and options that you *do* have.

The "That's Too Hard, I Can't or Don't Want to Do It"

I think this is the most common one. This is inertia at its core talking. Marshall Goldsmith speaks at length about inertia in his book, *Mojo*. Marshall shares that "Our default response in life is not to experience meaning or happiness. Our default response is to experience inertia." [70]

We are masters of talking ourselves out of things in order to stay in our inertia. This is becoming increasingly prevalent in this chaotic and busy life as we simply stop pushing against the tide and roll with the status quo.

Inertia is easier, more comfortable, safer, and requires less of us in the short term, so we sacrifice our long-term sparkle for short-term comfort. It takes a lot of emotional and mental energy to make a meaningful change in our lives.

Just think back to a version of yourself from five years ago. Are you that much different than you were back then? How much have you really changed? Are you more loving? More thoughtful? Have you made that health change you wanted to make?

Odds are, if you are like me, you have not changed that much. The truth is we get used to ourselves and our lives, and while we may not like our present circumstances, the platform isn't hot enough to cause us to jump and make a change. So, instead of putting in the energy to make the change, we stuff the idea down, make up some excuse in our head, find ourselves a new TV show to binge, and go back to our sparkle-stealing life on Monday.

The result: You stay comfortable, but you stay stuck.

The "That's Who I Am" Story

This is a powerful one with deep psychology underneath. This is a dynamic where we associate with the identity of the person we believe we are so much that we will do anything to retain it. Examples: I am an introvert or extrovert, I am a Democrat or Republican, I am creative or not creative, I am a writer, I am not a writer, I am, I am, I am. Often times, our roles in life and their corresponding identities take over our personal identities and slowly but surely we morph into the person we feel we should be to best meet the expectations of that role. For example, our role as a wife, mother, father, daughter, son, employee, etc.

The result: You will make decisions to match your perceived identity that are driven by your subconscious. That matching process and your identity can keep you stuck and keep you from exploring a part of yourself that could bring you tremendous joy.

The "I'm Not Ready" Story

This is one that women, in particular, often fall prey to. From my time in HR, women were, without question, most often the ones that would not raise their hand for a stretch job they did not meet *all* the qualifications for. They felt they didn't have enough experience and needed to keep "paying their dues." They also were least likely to negotiate their job offers. I often coached women who felt they needed to have all of the qualifications of a job description before they would be ready to compete for a role. Meanwhile, their male counterparts were not at all shy about asking, and sometimes demanding, to be put into a larger position, regardless of their qualifications.

I also find this dynamic in green personalities. We talked earlier about how greens are perfectionists. As a result, they believe they must be completely ready, with all of their checklist done and every ingredient in place, before they take a step. If this is you, this will hold you back from finding your flow and a groove that lights you up. To help your cause, adopt a blue friend if you don't already have one. Blues are fantastic at taking risks and swings, even when they are not ready. They know that they can fail fast, which is a methodology many R&D organizations have adopted. It's called an agile methodology, where you test an idea, try something, fail, learn, and keep moving. Life will rarely line up all the dominoes for you, and the stoplights will rarely ever all be green. You just have to jump.

The result: You will waste valuable time waiting for the stars to line up and may miss golden opportunities that were yours for the taking.

*****

These are just a few rut stories. There are plenty more. If you see yourself in these stories, you may have dug yourself into a hole. The good news is you just need to own it and face it to put your foot on the right path. You are doing that now just by reading this book. We will talk more about how to put this into motion at the end of the book.

THIEF 5: TIME and HURRY

"Time is a thief. It steals our memory, our hopes, our opportunities, and our strength, leaving us only with the sense that there is never enough of it."[71] We live in a highly overscheduled world. I know that comes as no surprise to you in this era of constant meetings, constant dings of our cell phones, constant emails, constant children's activities, constant requests for our time, and constant everything. It is a relentless and demanding pace that wears down even the most seasoned hard-work warriors. We are starved for time despite there being 1,440 minutes every day that replenishes itself every morning. We are hurried and buried in busy. Everything is rushed and everything is asap. "ASAP' has become a four-letter word to me now. If there isn't a life-or-death impact hanging in the balance, I check myself on the urgency. I have created too many five-alarm fires for myself in my life.

Now, in this season of life, I am slowing things down on purpose. One of my new favorite made-up words for myself is "unhurried." We all need less hurry and a little more "still."

We want time to be still and think. We want time to find our voice. We want time to be, to exercise, to eat our bowl of rocky road ice cream slowly, to play games with our kids, and we want time to just sit in silence.

We want time, and we want peace. I will admit there are times when I am in my car alone and thankful that I've gotten a red light because it gives me at least one minute to just sit and be. It's one minute of sanity and calm in a life of chaos that seems so unbalanced. Work-life balance is a term thrown around often and was the subject of many employee roundtables over the years I attended. It is an all-elusive question that everyone is seeking an answer to.

We all must define what it means for us in the season of life that we are in. Some people enjoy their work so much that they skew their balance more heavily on work and are just fine with that. That is okay for a short period, but I can tell you from experience that even a job you love will start to wear your sparkle down if you are too heavily focused on work.

Finding outlets of creativity, calm, or connection that bring you joy outside of work is critical. It will help you stay focused on the things that round you out and keep you centered in life. Otherwise, you risk having your exhaustion become a status symbol, and I promise that is not the kind of status you want.

For others, their imbalance and heavy weighting on work are not by choice, and it can start to feel as though your "have to" list is much larger than your "want to" list, which will create resentment within you. This can be especially challenging for parents of young children. A recent report in the *New York Times* states that 66% of parents of young children suffer from burnout. [72]

It is no surprise. The pull from home often comes at the same time that you are in the stride of your career, where the pull of your work is heavy and constant. As a result, you pay a heavy personal cost that sometimes feels completely unmanageable. The pandemic made this dynamic even more acute, and many parents' coping resources and coping reserves were completely depleted. You feel like you are giving, giving, giving, and giving both at work and at home, and there comes a time where you feel that you are at a breaking point.

It's important to think about where you can go and can ask for help. Whether it's from a spouse, family member, friend or maybe a neighbor...someone that can help you with even the lightest of duties to help ease your burden. Self-compassion, giving yourself grace and acknowledging that you just are going to do the best you can for this season of your life, and letting the chips fall where they may, also go a long way in helping reduce your stress.

Regardless of the situation you find yourself in, you will have to get more comfortable with setting boundaries in your life around where you spend your time.

You may think about work and home and find it very difficult to find anything you could say no to or anywhere that you could do things differently. Still, you would be surprised what possibilities open up when you are intentional and firm about creating the life you want.

Your manager may be more flexible than you think they might be. As a tip, think about what they want, what you want, and where the intersection is.

Think about what an "and equation" could be versus an "or equation." For example, you may want more flexibility in your working hours, so talk to your manager and explore the options. Maybe you could work fewer hours for a period of time or change the hours that you start and stop.

You don't know until you try, and the frantic pace of our lives will continue filling your calendar until you decide to take control.

You need time to reflect. You need time to think. You need time to breathe. You need time to consider what has happened to your sparkle and your plan of action. You cannot give away what you don't have. Remember the flight instructions to put on your oxygen mask before helping others. Time and space in this season of your life are oxygen. Breathe it in deeply and whenever you can. Breathe it in and use it to find the strength to light your own candle and shine bright for the world.

THIEF 6: LACK OF CONVICTION AND SLOPPY THINKING

Whenever we would start a significant change initiative in our organization, of all the questions we could choose to focus on first, we always focused on why. It wasn't what, when, how, or where. It was why. A strong why becomes the jet fuel when you are starting a transformation. It is also the backup battery when you feel you are running out of gas.

Understanding your why, and assessing your level of conviction against it, is a critical step in the process and is often a derailer if skipped. For example, I'll use my love/love (no hate in this relationship, that's for sure!) relationship with food and the years of stops and starts of healthy eating.

I always started with what I thought was a strong why in each attempt. Maybe it was because I didn't feel good, or I couldn't fit in my clothes, or perhaps it was because my cholesterol had gotten too high. There are many compelling reasons why I should want to lose weight and eat healthier.

Each time I would start, I would do well for a few weeks or months. Invariably at some point, the stress of a day or the lure of a freshly baked chocolate chip cookie would always get the best of me. And I'm an all-in or all-out kind of girl, so I'm either eating healthy or I'm not. There isn't a lot of middle ground for me.

There is a saying that says that "the severity of the itch is directly proportional to the reach." I think that is true, and while I would love to tell you that I had found a strong enough itch to trigger my long-term healthy eating, I'm still searching. So, I'm still "thinking about" eating healthy, and I'm still "working on it," but as you can tell, those are sloppy words and sloppy thoughts that I know will not get me anywhere.

My friend Sandy also taught me about this concept of sloppy words and sloppy thoughts, which ultimately create traps for you. Saying phrases like, "I am thinking about" ... "I am trying to" ... "I am working on" ... "I need to figure out how to" ... "I hope that...", "Yes, but...", are counterproductive to your goals and are indicative of a lukewarm conviction. As the great philosopher Yoda once said, "Do or do not do. There is no try."

We need to be crystal clear on our why and crystal clear on the degree to which it inspires us and calls us forward into action. We did not lose our sparkle overnight; it will take time and perseverance to get it back. We need to make sure we have absolute clarity on our why so we don't spin our wheels or lose momentum. Instead, we want to make slow but steady and sustainable progress. Our vocabulary then starts to sound much more like, "I am committed to" ... "I am choosing to" ... "I will do."

There is a quote by author Tracy Goss that says, "Change is a function of altering what you are *doing*, to improve something that is already possible in your reality (better, different, or more). Transformation is a function of altering how you are *being* in order to create something that is currently impossible in your reality." [73] I want you to own the possibilities in your life. I want you to be proud of who you are at your core and be able to translate that into a meaningful working life that lights you up. I want you to be fearless in stepping into a new chapter of your life. Be clear, be convicted, and be transformational.

THIEF 7: "SHOULD-ER" SYNDROME: SELF-DOUBT AND 'SHOULDING' ALL OVER YOURSELF

We all have a "little bitty shi**y committee"[74] playing songs of self-doubt in our mind every single day. We all have an annoying lead vocalist in the band who belts out lyric after lyric of unrealistic expectations and broken boundaries. I know the band so well that I know it has a trio of drums, bullhorns and an off-key piano. I got tired of it's tune so I've permanently fired them, they are no longer welcome. You have to shut yours down too, they are toxic to your dreams.

The seeds of self-doubt that we allow to be planted in our minds can stay dormant until just the moment when you feel like you are on to something, and then they very quickly sprout to the surface. They start to choke out our excitement and confidence with thoughts like, "Sure, you're good at that, but so is everyone else." "That's not really a gift or anything special." "No one will value that." Or "Who do you think you are? You haven't earned the right to chase anything. You still need to prove yourself."

These thoughts of self-doubt then combine with our "should system" that we discussed earlier, becoming a nasty combination. If you are a "should-er" like me, you are letting someone else's dreams, fears, or opinions drive the car of your life. You are operating out of someone else's framework and set of expectations, and over time, it will stifle your sparkle because you are operating out of a place that is not authentic to you. Every decision you make or don't make is made with *their* expectations front and center. Here is how some of our 'should self-talk' might sound, as described by Brené Brown: [75]

"You should care about making money, not meaning or chasing some crazy dream. Come back down to the real world with the rest of us."

"You're supposed to grow up and be a _____. Everyone is counting on it."

"Yeah, no kidding, everyone hates their job. You're supposed to hate your work. That's the definition of work."

"You can't have your cake and eat it too. You can do work you love or work that supports the people you love, but not both."

"You should have a job with a nice steady paycheck. What if you fail?" [76]

I would ask, "What if you don't?"

Stop shoulding and doubting all over yourself. We must start taking control of the messages we let run through our brains. We have to dig deep and think, "What is it that I am so afraid of? What is on my should list? Why is it there? Who says?" [77]

I can't help but think of something I once heard author Rachel Hollis say about this topic, "Don't let someone in the cheap seats have an expensive opinion in your life." Yessss.

We are too often our own worst enemies. Our rut stories keep us comfortable and keep us frozen. Ernest Hemingway once said, "there is nothing noble in being superior to your fellow man. True nobility is being superior to your former self." You are in competition with no one, let that free you.

THIEF 8: FEAR and TAR PITS

Gospel singer Zach Williams has a powerful song titled *Fear is a Liar* in his album *Chain Breaker*. I have parts of it taped up to my wall to look at when I feel the insidious creep of fear rising up the back of my neck or sinking deep into my soul.

So many of us find a major roadblock in the form of fear, and there are so many things we let ourselves fear that stand in our way of true transformation or progress. Here are a few of my greatest hits in the fear category: Fear of embarrassment, fear of failure, and fear that I'll fall short of some standard of perfection I have put on myself. Fear of stepping too far outside the norm or too far away from what people expect of me. Fear of trying, fear of not trying, fear of being alone, and fear of rejection. SO many fears.

There are plenty more I could mention. For example, many people suffer from a term called "imposter syndrome," [i] which is a deep-down fear that despite all of your skill and experience, you will be found out to be a fraud or that you don't know what you are talking about. This is far more common than you might think. I know people from all walks of life and all levels that suffer from this, including several CEOs. We are all just figuring things out as we go. We are all, in a sense, just "faking it till we make it."

Fear feels like a tar pit to me. Every time I fear something, I get stuck in it. Here are real, tangible examples from my life. Some are trivial, just for fun.

- I was afraid to fly for years, and instead of conquering it, I literally drove days to get to a work meeting rather than fly. I eventually kicked it because I just could not physically keep the driving up (and my cholesterol was screaming from all the fast food).

- I was afraid of getting my ears pierced and, as a result, wore clip earrings until I was 25 when I finally bit the bullet. What a new and glorious world it was to have real earrings!

- I was afraid to quit my job because I was afraid of who I was without it. As I mentioned before, I had wrapped my entire identity around my career, so it was a terrifying thought. Leaving turned out to be the best decision I've ever made, and I wish I had done it five years earlier.

- I am afraid this book will fail, so I have spent the last three days coming up with just the right sub-title and have been stuck in an endless loop of overthinking. Thank goodness for my husband, who finally got tired of hearing my hemming and hawing and pushed me to make a choice. I literally was stuck in place and couldn't finish the book until I got this step done. My mind and fingers felt like they were caked in tar, and I couldn't work through it because I was afraid. Fear can be paralyzing.

I could keep going, but you get the point. Fear will talk you right out of your dreams and keep you from trying. It will keep you playing defense vs. offense, and will rob you from the life you were meant to have. Don't let it. Recognize you have the fear, fire the "itty bitty sh--- committee," tell it out loud to take a hike, enlist help and make at least one baby step in the direction you want to go. Every step will strengthen you and unleash your power to conquer this formidable foe. As Franklin D. Roosevelt once said, "the only thing to fear is fear itself."

CHAPTER SUMMARY ACTIVITY

****

Reflect through the sources of sparkle stealers and pick out the two that you feel are most relevant to you in this season of your life. Put those in the blanks below and then list one to two specific things that you can do to prevent them.

REFLECTION QUESTIONS

*The two biggest sparkle stealers in my life are _____ and _____.

*To combat them, I will:

_____

_____

_____

_____

CHAPTER REFLECTION NOTES

_____

_____

_____

_____

_____

_____

CHAPTER 15

POWER TOOL – REST

"Sometimes it's important to work for that pot of gold. But other times, it's essential to take time off and ensure that your most important decision in the day simply consists of choosing which color to slide down on the rainbow." ~Douglas Pagels

Can I just say how much writing this particular chapter makes my body relax and my inner introvert feel like she's in her warm, happy place?

I recently spoke to a friend who left a great job to take, as she describes it, "an intermission."

I love the word intermission as an analogy for this important stage of our lives. I'm so proud of her for recognizing her need for it and doing something about it. She is taking six months off, and when I asked her what was giving her the most excitement about this season of her life, she said, "What is exciting me is sleep. I feel like I just completed ten ironman triathlons. I'm completely depleted. Right now, I'm all about my cats, my jammies, and my couch."

Love that. We all have those moments when we need to find our physical and emotional couch. We all need that warm cozy set of pajamas to slide into and the space and time to pull the covers over our heads. We all need the love and comfort of a caring friend or the snuggle and cold nose of a beloved pet to curl up beside.

Consider these questions below for a moment:

- Do you often feel tired when you wake up in the morning?

- Having difficulty concentrating?

- Are your emotions easily affected by the actions of others?

- Have headaches, muscle aches, or generalized fatigue with no known medical diagnosis?

- Do you depend on quick energy fixes like caffeine or sugar to help you get through the day?

You will likely answer yes to some or all of these questions in a particular season of your life. When you do, it's a signal. It's part of the "It Is Time" calculation. Higher score = higher chance that it is time for you to consider a change and consider how you can get true rest.

In her book *Sacred Rest*, author and board-certified physician Dr. Saundra Dalton-Smith, takes us into her journey of burnout and her research on rest.

If you are interested, I highly recommend getting her book and reading the whole thing. I devoured it in one setting and found it helpful, refreshing, and restorative. When we hear the word rest, we automatically think about physical rest. That is just one part of the equation, though.

From Saundra's research, there are seven different kinds of rest that we need as humans to operate at our best and brightest on a sustainable basis. It gives us a road map to healing and a pathway to sparkle and serenity.

Dr. Dalton-Smith describes the start of her journey in the first chapter. I felt this description deep in my bones.

"There should be a "Get Out of Your Responsibilities Card" you can play on those days when life is just too difficult, days when everything within you wants a moment simply to be still. That thought flitted through my mind as I lay stretched out on the foyer floor.

The weight of an unexamined life flies heavy against the heart of the weary, pushing and pushing until it nudges you right past sanity..

I never realized the many facets of peace and rest that are available when you lay yourself down on purpose. Peace comes in many forms. On this day, it came in a 10-minute reprieve in the middle of the chaos that had become my life. There was no time to break away and do it right. No time for any long, drawn-out me-time ritualistic activities. No mani-pedi. No hot tea and biscuits. No caramel macchiato. No Dead Sea salt-infused bath.

I stretched out my back against the boards, palms down, and closed my eyes. In that moment of focused ceasing, I felt the beginning of peace stir within my body. Peace came slowly. It was as if God himself breathed the divine exhalation, releasing new strength into me. [78]

In our culture of hustle and cult of achievement, we believe that if we aren't doing something, then we are falling behind or wasting time. Doing is the prize. Rest has become the punishment.

Rest is not for the faint of heart. It means saying no. It means saying no to ourselves. It means saying no to others. It takes courage to rest in our very outcome-driven culture.

Our bodies crave true rest and if you don't get it, you will wake up feeling exhausted and go to bed feeling exhausted. We often think of rest as just the absence of activity, and we feel like if we get a good six, seven, or eight hours of sleep at night, we should be fine, yet we still have this feeling of "I am tired." It might even frustrate us because we may be fortunate enough to get good sleep, but we can't shake the tired feeling.

If that is you, there is a good chance that it is because you are mentally, emotionally, or spiritually tired. There is a difference between sleep and rest. Your mind, heart, and body are craving different rest. It's something in your heart, body, or mind that is drained, tired, or has reached the end of its rope, and it will be hard to shake the tired feeling until you identify what that "thing" is.

"What kind of tired are you?" Saundra asks, and then she goes on to describe that there are seven different kinds of rest: physical, mental, spiritual, emotional, social, sensory, and creative. Saundra describes in detail the symptoms of deficits in each area along with remedies in her book, so I won't cover those here. We'll just do a high-level view so you become aware of the key areas.

PHYSICAL REST (i.e., Sleep)

I don't know if you're like me, but it seems like every time I finish a major project, or on the first few days of my vacation, I either get sick or go into a three-day coma.

Our bodies are amazing creations, but they were not designed for the pace of life that we try to put them through. Your adrenaline will only take you so far. At the first opportunity, your body will find a way to shut itself down. It will grab you by the shoulders, look squarely in your eyes and push you right down to the ground.

According to the National Sleep Foundation, 45% of Americans say that poor or insufficient sleep affects their daily activities at least once per week. Over eight million people in the U.S. struggle to fall asleep and stay asleep.[79] I was, and still am at times, in that number. I, like clockwork, used to wake up at 4:30 a.m. every night and stare at the ceiling until about 6:30 a.m., when the annoying sound of my alarm goes off.

It had become such an expected part of my evening that I started planning what I would think about in those hours so that I could at least use the time productively.

You may have heard about the five stages of sleep. The goal is to get through all five to the REM (rapid-eye-movement) stage and stay there for about 20% of the night. High-quality sleep, when your brain stops actively processing, begins at stage three, and you enter a calm state.[80] While I haven't used one myself, many of my friends highly recommend the use of the Oura™ ring to give you powerful insights about your sleep health. It monitors several different biometrics to give you a daily morning reading of your readiness for the day and has been eye opening to many people I know.

Calm, stillness and quiet are what your mind and body crave. For many people though, stillness can create feelings ranging from overwhelming boredom to sheer panic. When things are still, they can feel uncertain and ambiguous. The only things we have to fill in the void and the quiet are the thoughts in our heads and the emotions in our hearts, and for many of us that's the last thing we want to hear.

Giving yourself time and space though for quiet can be incredibly restorative. As Saundra says, "it's time to exchange the daily hustle for the daily hush." [81]

MENTAL REST

My mind regularly feels like my computer browser with 18 different tabs open that I'm constantly toggling between, and it's exhausting. I can feel the little hamsters in my head panting. We clutter and overload our minds repeatedly, and while the mind is an amazing instrument, it can dance and dart around like my 5-year-old niece at her first ballet recital.

If you want to feel this dynamic, try doing your first session of meditation and try winning the game of mental whack-a-mole that your mind is so skilled at. Quieting your mind and not letting the racing thoughts that dart in from nowhere distract you is a learned skill.

Your brain is awash with mental noise. It's full of to-do list noise, planning noise, what-if noise, second-guessing noise, news noise, self-critique noise, work noise, judging noise, dreaming noise, and several other flavors of noise. In addition, if you are in a job that requires a lot of creativity, academic thought, or large amounts of strategic thinking, you will need more rest.

For me, doing an evening "mind dump" helps. It helps me get everything out of my head and calm the noise inside. If you want to try it, put a notebook beside your bed, and 15 minutes before you go to bed, write down all the things that are rolling around in your head and close the notebook.

Meditation can also be a powerful antidote. I know all my red type A's will cringe at this one, but it has been proven to be powerful in creating calm and rest in the most chaotic of lives. There are tons of apps and online tutorials about how to meditate (Headspace™ is one I've heard good feedback on), but the essence is you are giving yourself a few minutes each day to focus your thoughts and clear your mind.

EMOTIONAL REST

Emotional rest deficits can come from two different sources. One involves giving too much, and one involves saying too little.

We all have an emotional bank account, and some of us give freely out of this account to others at the expense of our emotional health. We give and give and give, and we care and care and care until we get to the place where we are just emotionally exhausted and have nothing left to give. We take so many for the team that we don't have any left to take for ourselves.

For others of us, we spend our emotional dollars on negative emotions. We easily and generously hand out anger to the sports car driver that cuts us off on our morning commute. We give out frustration to a coworker during a conflict, or we may even hand out searing criticisms to ourselves regularly.

All of these emotional expenditures deplete the account and tax the reserves. Negative emotions come with a double tax and deplete our reserves even faster. If we want to keep giving, we have to restore our accounts. We cannot give what we don't have.

Others of us store up toxic emotions deep in the recesses of our minds like a squirrel burying nuts for the winter, and we never let them see the light of day.

This, much like the battery on your computer, drains your power while you aren't looking. We store them and hide these negative emotions, that is until we are given the permission and freedom to let them peek their heads out. When they do, they often come screaming out of the gate with floods of tears and healing. I have experienced this dynamic firsthand with hundreds of employees that attended a leadership training class that I conducted dozens of times over the years.

One of the class activities is designed to accelerate team bonding and enable team members to see each other as humans. This allows everyone to give each other more grace in the day-to-day workplace. For the exercise, we have the students create a line graph of their lives and chart out the highs and lows in their life with dots above and below a neutral line.

First, without exception, everyone takes more time than their allotted five minutes to share. I give them about 20 minutes to complete the graph and then tell them that they will have five minutes to pick out a couple of items to share with the group. They begin to share, and it is common for it to go 15 to 20 minutes because they find the process of sharing is healing without them even realizing it.

Second, and most importantly, there is almost always a challenge in their life that has triggered them to bury an emotion. They find this is the first time they have felt an opportunity and safe space to talk about it, despite it being a work setting (sometimes it is easier to tell people we don't know our deepest secrets).

At first, the honesty and vulnerability were shocking and, frankly, a little uncomfortable. In the beginning, I didn't always know the best way to react. I learned over time that the best thing I could do was just to let them talk, be a listening ear and offer support in the form of a hug or compassionate eye contact.

This exercise consistently ranked as one of the most impactful team-building sessions that participants attended, and there were always incredibly high levels of teaming after these events.

We are not designed to keep our emotions bottled up. We are designed to live in community and do life together, we are designed to share and connect.

What Can Help:
Audit Your Circle

Think of the people you surround yourself with and the type of emotions they most often give off. The mirror neurons in our brain tend to mimic those that we are around. Are there people that make you feel drained after you have interacted with them? Did you start the day in a good mood but encounter someone that changed your mood?

Do you dread being in the presence of certain people? If so, consider the nature of your relationship and the amount of time you are around them. Find ways to counterbalance their effect by adding more people in your circle with strong positive and optimistic vibes. Keep people in your life who help you reveal and release your best self.

Emotional Intelligence

Study your own emotions like a science project. Notice how you react during the day to specific situations and contemplate why. Know what the triggers of certain emotions are for you. Avoid the triggers that are negative and double down on the positive triggers.

Stop Side-Eyeing

As we discussed before, stopping yourself from comparing yourself to others will give you a massive lift in this area. Become more comfortable and even proud of your personality and who you are.

Think of the situations or people that most often cause you to act inauthentically or to compare yourself. Try to identify what it is within you that you are compensating for, flip the script, and embrace it.

Find Your Person

Everyone needs to have a person in their life that they can confide in, cry with, vent to, share the ups and downs of their lives with, and be vulnerable enough with to share those toxic emotions that cause us so much pain.

This might be a spouse or a best friend, but it could also be, and may need to be, someone like a therapist or a coach. If there is someone in your life that you trust to be this person for you, then thank them and tell them you may need them more in the future and why and offer your listening ear in return.

SENSORY REST

Imagine for a moment you are sitting on the beach. You hear the lapping of the waves, you feel the sand under your toes, you smell your cold and refreshing pineapple pina colada beside you, you feel the warmth of the sun, and you are nodding into blissful oblivion. Suddenly, you hear the dreaded but familiar ding of your text messages or the ring of your phone, and you are snapped back to reality. That is not the sound you wanted to hear at that moment, and you cannot stop yourself from looking at your phone.

It was a message from work, and now for the next three hours, your brain will subconsciously be processing that message even though you have now turned your phone off.

We are overloaded with stimulation. We have an innumerable amount of telephone chirps, rings and dings, a constant buzz of electronics, a well-intended background of elevator music playing, a glaring artificial light penetrating our eyes, smells of every kind of food imaginable, flashing billboards, automatic toilet flushes, overhead announcements, fluorescent overhead lights, artificial air fresheners, overly loud commercials, and tugging children and puppies on our pant legs, just to name a few of the intrusions to our senses daily.

The introvert in me is easily overwhelmed by this. You can ask my husband. I need to have frequent moments in a week where I sit in complete stillness and complete quiet. I feel like my brain might explode if I hear, smell, or see one more thing. Quiet is one of my favorite words, and it makes my heart smile. I seek it out and stop at my local bookstores and libraries to look for quiet spaces, but even those sacred spaces are no longer quiet.

They are filled with the whirl of coffee grinders, the laughter of teenagers talking about last night's party, or someone once again talking on their phone in speaker mode for the whole world to hear. It has gotten so bad that I have thought of opening a place and naming it simply Quiet. It would be a safe place with little sensory stimulation and a lot of quiet (basically every extrovert's nightmare).

If you are a green personality or introverted, you are likely at higher risk for overload in this area. Do a gut check for yourself to see if you crave quiet. If so, find ways to unplug (literally and figuratively).

CREATIVE REST

Our souls crave beauty. Whether it is in viewing a beautiful sunset, feeling the rain on our face, seeing a baby's smile, beholding an inspiring work of art, or hearing music that tickles our ears, we seek beauty and light.

We want to be captivated, we want to be inspired, we want to be amazed, and we want to feel part of something greater. It's why we love it so much when we have a chance to soak in the beauty of the Grand Canyon, smell the scent of pine trees in the forest, or listen to a captivating symphony. We need this beauty and rest in our lives to counterbalance all of the negativity and toxicity we are bombarded with every day.

Explore nature and art and find the one you feel most drawn to and captivated by. For me, it's water and the beach. For you, it may be mountains, ski slopes, art studios, deserts, or symphonies. Find a way to experience and be around it on a more frequent and regular basis. For me, I make sure that at least once a month I make a road trip to a body of water. In the fall, I find parks to walk in where there are leaves that I can step on and crunch amid bright, colorful, beautiful trees.

Find new things in nature for your eyes to feast on and build new memories from. Build mini-sabbaticals into your life. It may be an hour, a day, a week, or some other period, but schedule time for yourself to be in the presence of the things that inspire you.

SOCIAL REST

We crave connection and in our increasingly socially connected world, we are becoming lonelier by the day. In a recent study, 36% of all Americans—including 61% of young adults and 51% of mothers with young children, feel "serious loneliness." [82]

Loneliness is a formidable enemy and can lead to early mortality and a wide array of serious physical and emotional problems, including depression, anxiety, heart disease, and substance abuse. In addition, our bodies crave physical touch. [83]There is a medical term to describe its deficit, touch starvation. Touch is a potent stress reducer that reduces the cortisol in our bodies.

Touch can calm heart palpitations, anxiety, and blood pressure by stimulating pressure receptors that send signals to the vagus nerve. It then stimulates pathways for oxytocin, the natural antidepressant serotonin, and the pleasure neurotransmitter dopamine. [84] Regardless of whether you are introverted or extroverted, you crave connection with others.

One recent study of over 300,000 people found that loneliness increases the risk of premature death by 50% across all causes and is equivalent to the risk of smoking a pack of cigarettes every day.[85] Perhaps we need a surgeon general's warning for loneliness as well.

Whether it's someone looking you in your eyes and really seeing you, touching your hand, the warmth of a hug, someone laughing at your joke, a compliment from a coworker, or the help needed request from a friend that makes you feel needed, having a connection to other humans is a vital part of our story of rest. The need for recognition and being seen by others is one of our deepest human needs, and that comes through connection with others.

Connections that are physical and present. Connections that are real and sincere. You can be surrounded by people and still feel incredibly lonely. Just ask the young mom that suddenly lost her husband but is surrounded by dozens of friends. Or the social media maven with 1,000 friends but no one to call. It is all too easy in this world to feel invisible.

Attention and presence are some of the greatest gifts you can give to another human. Just ask the scruffy and disheveled-looking homeless person that you speed by every day. You think they want money, but what they really want is for you to look them in the eye, ask them their name, and hear their story. I bet they would let you keep your donated change in exchange for a few minutes of your time.

To help us fuel our inner cravings for social rest, it's important to find your people. Find that friend that gets you, and you can be your whole self around (and won't judge when you cancel the lunch for the third time or come out wearing two different earrings). Find people in your circle, or that you can add to your circle, that you can be yourself with and who are positive, encouraging, and uplifting to you. Choose real face time versus technology time. Join a social, community, civic, hobby, or religious group to find like-minded souls to be around. Join a cause that you feel enthusiastic about. Get a new pet that you can touch and snuggle with in lonely moments. If you are introverted, focus on a few strong relationships versus many. The important part is to make an effort and find your tribe.

SPIRITUAL REST

I have moved the last category of rest, spiritual rest, to the Appendix. Not because it's an afterthought but because it may be the most important thought. That said, I also recognize that it may take you into a different category of thoughts and will offer a distinct set of questions for you to reflect on.

For now, we will stay centered on the types of rest you are most familiar with. At a high level, consider spiritual rest to be the kind of rest you need to create a stronger connection to the divine for yourself.

My guess is you instinctively know whether this is an area of needed focus for you. Whether it is or not, I would encourage you to read that portion of the Appendix once you've finished with the main part of the book. I believe you will find an opportunity to do deep reflection in this area that can be healing and inspiring to your soul.

*****

Journalist Sydney J. Harris once said, "The best time to rest is when you don't have time for it." Truer words were never spoken. We will never feel like we have time to rest. We will never feel like we have time to find our sparkle. We will think this all sounds great, and then chances are we'll put this book down and go back to life as we lived it.

Don't let that be your story. Don't let that be your outcome. Rest like you have earned it, because you have.

CHAPTER SUMMARY ACTIVITY

****

REFLECTION QUESTIONS

Reflect on the types of rest we've talked about in the chapter and identify the top two to three that you feel you have the most need for. Use that to fill in the blanks.

The types of rest I most need to feel healthy and restored are
_____, _____, and _____.

I will do the following two things in the next two weeks to help bring me back in balance:

CHAPTER REFLECTION NOTES

_____

_____

_____

_____

_____

_____

_____

CHAPTER 16

POWER TOOLS:

QUESTIONS and BOUNDARIES

You may have noticed that I love questions. I find them immensely helpful. I collect questions and keep a list of many of them in a notebook that I use to reflect on how my life is going and how I am feeling.

Here is a list of many questions I have collected over the years. Feel free to use them as you'd like to help you in your thinking now or in the future. I use different questions in different seasons and for different reasons. All these questions I have stolen proudly from books I have read or from great mentors I have had along the way. As Tony Robbins says, "quality questions create a quality life."

Tony Robbins – *Awaken the Giant Within* [86]
Our experience in life is based on what we focus on. Tony lists a set of questions to ask ourselves in the morning and the evening to help our focus. He recommends that if you have difficulty answering the question, replace or add the word "could." For example, "What *could* I be most happy about in my life right now?"

Morning Power Questions:
- What am I happy, excited, proud, or grateful about in my life now? (Or what *could* I be happy, excited, or proud about?)
- What am I enjoying the most in my life right now?

- What am I committed to in my life right now? How does that make me feel?
- Who do I love? Who loves me?

Evening Power Questions:
- What have I given today?
- What did I learn today?
- How has today added to the quality of my life, or how can I use today as an investment in my future?

Sandy Sullivan, The Alchemy Group
- Who do you inspire? What do you inspire? Who inspires you? What inspires you?
- Who and what do you breathe life into?
- What is and is not working for you right now?
- How well do you know when something isn't working, and who will you talk to?
- Where is my learning coming from right now? What I know, what I don't know, or what I know I don't know?
- What have you tried so far? What has been most successful? What has been surprising?
- What assumptions are you making? What questions do you need to ask? Who would you ask a question of, and what would the question be? What is the next right step?
- Who do you choose to be? What is your new brand? What is the one thing you need to start doing? What is the one thing you need to stop doing?
- Does your current vision for yourself empower you? Inspire you? Call you forward into action? Excite you? Support your aliveness, joy, and well-being?
- What do you yearn for? What do you crave?

Gregg Thompson, in his book, *Unleashed! Leader as Coach* [87]
- What matters most to you right now?
- In which traits and characteristics do you take the most pride?

- What important thing have you learned about yourself recently?
- What excites you most about your future?
- For what do you want to be known?
- Where have you achieved your greatest successes? When you are at your best, what are you doing?
- Are you currently doing your best work?
- What is the most exciting outcome you could imagine?
- What one personal change will result in the biggest benefit?
- If you felt powerful and in control, what would be possible?
- What is an entirely different way to see your situation?
- What thoughts and habits are no longer serving you well?
- What actions do you need to take that you are avoiding?
- How can you change your job to do more of the things you love?
- What specific outcomes are you expecting? What will be different this time?
- Which difficult conversation needs to happen?
- What is the most potent first step? What short-term breakthroughs are necessary?
- What help do you need from others?
- Do you trust yourself to follow through? What promises are you making to yourself?
- How will you know when you are on the new road?
- What will you do when you encounter unexpected obstacles?

Questions force us to look inside for the answers that we already have within ourselves. It's one thing for someone just to tell you that you need to do something (lose weight, for example). It's entirely different when you go through a process in which you end up telling yourself the same thing. That process often involves questions. If you ever engage with a coach, they will ask you many great questions. Their currency is questions.

So, coach yourself like the champion you are. Ask yourself great questions, and let the hard ones hang with you. Let them marinate. Let them inspire you. Let them guide you.

BOUNDARIES

Boundaries are beautiful. They represent strength and clarity. They represent inspiration and freedom.

We have for too long viewed boundaries as weakness or as inflexibility. We want to help, we want to give, and we want to make a difference. So we blur the boundaries and blow through the caution lights. We give and give of ourselves until we are running entirely on fumes and day-old french fries.

We *need* boundaries to keep us balanced, whole, and sparkly. Think of them as life's vegetables. We may not love them, but your body craves them, and your health pays the price without them. You may even find you start to crave them once you get used to them (ok, maybe not Brussels sprouts, but you get the point).

Like vegetables, boundaries come in all shapes and sizes. There can be boundaries on your time, the people you let into your life, the topics you'll talk about, the lines you won't cross, and the types of work you'll do or won't do. There are financial boundaries, physical boundaries, and emotional boundaries. There are boundaries you may find hard to honor and boundaries you are afraid to put in place.

Example:

In her book *Untamed*, Glennon Doyle talks about a key boundary that is difficult to put in place but may be what you need, which is relationship boundaries.[88] Here is a fun exercise. Imagine winning the lottery and being given an island (wouldn't that be cool?).

This island is uninhabited and is waiting for you to do exactly what you want to with it. You get to make all the rules. You decide what flavor margaritas you'll drink on Mondays, how many hammocks versus beach chairs you'll have, and, importantly, who you will allow on the island and when. Glennon goes through this exercise in the book and has you think about this concept of having a "safe island."

This island is full of people that fit your values, give you joy, and make you a better person. They get an all-access pass to your island; they just need to let you know when they are coming. Now imagine that your island also has a drawbridge. You decide when and why you let the drawbridge down for the other people in your life that may not bring you joy. If they are sparkle stealers, maybe the bridge needs to stay up more than it comes down. High performance executive coach Dan Pena once said, "show me your friends and I'll show you your future." [89] What a powerful reflection point.

*****

CHAPTER SUMMARY ACTIVITY

****

REFLECTION QUESTIONS

From the list in the chapter or from other questions you may already have, write down two powerful questions you believe you need to ask yourself consistently over the next week.

Question 1:

Question 2:

BOUNDARIES REFLECTION QUESTION

Give some thought to our earlier thinking about sparkle stealers from Chapter 14.

Consider if there are people, situations, events, environments, mindsets, tendencies, or uses of your time that may need boundaries. Think about why, when, where, and how you could implement them and what your next steps need to be.

CHAPTER REFLECTION NOTES

CHAPTER 17

POWER TOOL – SYSTEMS

S ystems make the world go around. We have operating systems, defense systems, financial systems, educational systems, weight loss systems, information systems, ecological systems, and the list goes on. We use systems to remind us, guide us, and inform us. We use them to enable us to achieve a goal, to support us, help us scale, help us communicate, and sometimes help save us from ourselves.

As you go through this process of finding and reclaiming your sparkle, be sure to spend time thinking about the kinds of systems you need and how you will put them into place. As well-intended but busy, impatient, and impulsive humans, we need systems to keep us strong and on our path. For me, I need both warning systems and support systems. At a minimum, these are two systems that you may also need.

SUPPORT SYSTEMS

Fighting burnout is a team sport. Instead of trying to gut it out on your own or calling up your inner gritty gremlins, take a moment to pause and connect with people who can help you in the fight and help you in your journey. If you are a card-carrying member of the "I'll figure this out myself" club, tear up your membership card. This is not the time. While you and you alone have to own the decisions you make, you need a team to help you pull it off.

We all need support. From the strongest red in the room, who is fiercely independent and asks for help only as a last resort, to the humble yellow, who needs the encouragement and the support of others as much as they do oxygen, we all need support. You need that person who can be your champion and cheerleader. You need that person in your life that can be your truth-teller. You need that person who can hold you up when you feel like you can't take one more step.

Consider the kind of support you have engaged in other situations. Maybe it was a support system you created when you were trying to lose weight. Or maybe it was a grief support system when you lost a loved one, or maybe there is a young mom's support system in your community that you are plugged into.

Think about the kinds of support you find most valuable and that work for you and your personality. The kind of support I need as a red, very independent personality is different than the kind you may need if you have a different personality style. It's not a one-size-fits-all approach, so spend a few minutes and think about what you need to support you in this journey. Think about the kinds of people you need in your life and the kinds of people you don't need. Think about the resources you may need to have available to you or the information you may need to have access to regularly.

Here are some ideas:

Types of roles you need people to play for you in your life based on your personality type. If you know you are not strong or have an allergy to a specific behavior, then that may be the kind of support you need most in this journey.

- A cheerleader, your constant source of encouragement, and a compassionate ear.
- A champion, someone who will advocate for you.
- An organizer to help you organize your thoughts or help you plan.
- A driver (not literally). This is more of a person that has a driven personality that can help give you a kick in the pants when you need it.

- An innovator that can help you see things from a different angle and spark a new idea for you.
- A truth-teller who will give you direct, honest, and objective feedback and tell you when you may be veering off the path.
- A mentor, someone who has already been there and done that. For example, suppose you are planning to start your own business. In that case, you may need someone who has already begun that same business and is several years ahead.

Part of your support system could even leverage technology and be an app. For example, many apps can send you daily reminders or daily inspirational messages to help keep you on your path. You will know best what you need, so use this as an opportunity to set yourself up for success. Identify and create your support systems before you need them.

WARNING SYSTEMS

Even with the most powerful of support systems, you will find that early warning systems can be highly effective. If you are a hard-charging red that goes ninety miles an hour down a path and doesn't stop to look at what might be coming, you need a warning system.

For the green that gets so into the weeds and the details that they lose sight of the bigger picture, to the yellow who is eternally optimistic and doesn't see where things may go wrong, you need a warning system. Or to the blue that is so full of passion that they don't think about the structure or processes needed that could keep them from tripping, you also need a warning system.

Warning systems give us a chance to correct ourselves before we veer too far off our path into a danger zone. They can grab us by the shoulders and shake us, beep in our ears until we pay attention, flash in our faces until we look their way, or stop us in our tracks when we are headed in the wrong direction.

A warning system could be a friend, a coach, or an accountability metric you monitor. It could be the achievement of a milestone that tells you you're making progress. It could be an outcome you expect and look for or a side effect that you anticipate. It could be a checklist or a to-do list that you diligently work through, a reminder you set on your phone, or anything in between.

I have a friend who knows that she will only make progress if she has an accountability partner. So, she has a friend that graciously agreed to serve in that role for her. At the end of every day, my friend calls her accountability partner, and she asks her a pre-determined set of questions. Her accountability partner doesn't necessarily have to hear the answers. It's the process of her knowing that she has someone who will expect her to call every day and to hear positive progress, which keeps her focused on her goal.

I once asked a coworker to be my truth-teller. I gave them permission to pull me aside and have a little prayer meeting with me when they observed me behaving in a way I said I didn't want to. Someone else I know, who has a big green personality and is highly analytical, created an incredibly detailed spreadsheet. The spreadsheet lists every step she needs to take to lead her from her current point to her end state.

She gave herself a timeline for each step and held herself accountable to that timeline and to accomplish each of those micro steps.

Whatever works best for you, use it. It will be a key piece in your success formula.

****

CHAPTER SUMMARY ACTIVITY

****

REFLECTION QUESTIONS

The two elements I most need in my support system are
_____ and _____

The one way I will give myself an early warning system is that I will

CHAPTER REFLECTION NOTES

_____

_____

_____

_____

_____

_____

_____

CHAPTER 18

POWER TOOL – VISIONS and GOALS

I n full transparency, if you work in the corporate world and hear the word goals and make a silent cringe, so do I. Frankly, the whole goal-setting process frustrated me, and I dreaded it every year.

We would spend an endless number of hours discussing our strategy and then make an overly complicated set of goals that had to cascade throughout the organization.

Despite many attempts to make them simple, "smart", and inspiring, we always fell short. The red driver in me just wanted to set one truly clear and crisp goal that the whole organization could see themselves in, and we focus on just that one thing for the year, but that was just never in the cards.

The good news is we can make our own rules now. I am not opposed to goals, I'm just averse to complicated processes around goals. I love dreams, and I love plans, and goals are the bridge between the two. Napoleon once said , "a goal is just a dream with a deadline." I like that.

The goal of this goals section (pun intended) is for you to decide and set one goal that inspires you and pulls you into the future you are craving. It may be a small baby step goal, or it may be a monster transformational vision. Still, you would not be reading this book and have made it this far if there wasn't something in your soul that wanted to change.

You've been given a lot to think about so far. We will do a couple more activities to help you crystallize your thoughts and turbocharge your inner dreamer and planner. Ms. Red, who is tired of the platitudes and wants action, I hear you. I see you, Mr. Blue, whose brain has been sparkling with ideas the whole time you've been reading this. Mr. Green, whose favorite thing in the world is a well-thought-out, spreadsheet-charted plan, this chapter is for you. And Ms. Yellow, who wants to call her best friend and share all about it, I see you too. We will all be able to take this forward and gain the momentum we eagerly desire.

ACTIVITY: YOUR GOALS

Let's spend some time now and do some dreaming in the context of goals. It will give your brain a boost of energy and get your creative juices flowing. The plan is to make it simple and even a little fun. For reference, Tony Robbins talks about this topic in his book, *Awaken the Giant Within*. Some of the content is taken from there if you want to grab it and read it in more detail. Tony describes the start of his own journey below:

"Eight years ago, I did an exercise that created a future so compelling that my whole life changed as a result. As part of the overall process of raising my standards, I established a whole new set of goals, writing down all the things I would no longer settle for, as well as what I was committed to having in my life. I set aside all my limiting beliefs and sat down on the beach with my journal. I wrote continuously for three hours, brainstorming every possibility of what I could ever imagine doing, being, having, creating, experiencing, or contributing.

The timeline I gave myself for achieving these goals was anytime from tomorrow to the next 20 years. I never stopped to think whether I could achieve these goals or not. I simply captured any possibility that inspired me and wrote it down. I considered what kind of person I would have to be and what things I would need to accomplish by nine years from now,

eight years, seven years, and so on, reaching back until today. What
specific action could I take today that would lead me on the road to the
destiny of my choice? On that day, I set specific goals that transformed
my life. " [90]

Thinking twenty years ahead may seem too overwhelming to you at this stage. I know it was for me. Life changes so fast that I tend not to use a long-term timeline. Instead, I decide what and how it is I want to be in this life and the impact I want to make, and then I plan out one tactical step I can take in the next month to get me there. The following month, I pick another. Baby steps lead to giant leaps. So, choose whatever time frame feels most appropriate for your situation. The important part is to articulate the future that you want for yourself.

STEP 1: PERSONAL DEVELOPMENT GOALS

Grab an empty notebook. Write at the top of the page Personal Development Goals.

Next, let your mind freely roam and think about everything you would like to accomplish in your life that relates to your personal growth. There are no right or wrong answers, the key here is to write in a very free-flowing manner for at least 5 minutes, and it may go much longer than that.

Write down anything and everything you can imagine, regardless of the timeline. It could be something you want to do next week, next year, or in the next decade. Channel your inner child or your vacationing self who is relaxing on the beach and daydreaming. Be crazy with it; don't limit timelines, financial resources, available time, etc. Pretend the entire world is your oyster.

Here are some questions that may help get you thinking:
- What did you want to be when you grew up? What did you want to learn?
- What did you want to know more about? What would you like to learn?

- What are the skills you want to master? What is a character trait you want to develop?
- What might you want to do for your physical well-being? Get a weekly massage? Get physically fit? Learn to cook vegetarian? Run a marathon?
- Conquer your fear of flying? Learn to speak French? Study archaeology in Egypt?
- Learn to dance? Learn to play the piano?

The possibilities are endless.

STEP 2: TO BE OR TO BRING GOALS

Write down words describing what you want to be in this life. For example, I have always wanted to be witty and funny and to be able to make people laugh. I'm not sure I'm wired that way, but we can all dream, right?

Examples: I want to be kind, patient, funny, inspiring, etc.

Or consider what it is you want to bring to this world. What is missing in our world?

Examples: I want to bring more kindness, more humor, more inspiration, more accuracy, more collaboration, etc.

STEP 3: TO EXPERIENCE GOALS

What are those things you want to experience in this life?

Examples: Attend the opening of a Broadway play? A film premiere? Pitch in the World Series? Climb Mount Everest? Take your mom to Hawaii? Star in a ballet? Sail around the world? Scuba dive in the Caribbean? Meditate in a Buddhist monastery?

Let your imagination run wild.

STEP 4: FINANCIAL OR CAREER GOALS

What do you want from things that bring you financial gain (ex career, investments, etc)?

Examples: Do you want to lead large teams? Do you want to be the next Bill Gates? Do you want to get a patent? Do you want to be a CEO? What kind of impact do you want to have? Do you want to be able to take a nice vacation every year? Do you want to put your kids through college with no loans? Do you want to start a business? Do you want to take a business public?

STEP 5: CONTRIBUTION GOALS

This can be a compelling category because this is where you think about the mark you want to leave and the difference you make in the lives of others. Think about what you want to bring to this world and what you want the world to have more of. It could be something simple like committing to a recycling program or as large as starting a nonprofit.

Examples: Help build a shelter for the homeless, adopt a child, volunteer at a soup kitchen, read to the blind, visit someone in prison, volunteer in the Peace Corps, take balloons to nursing homes, help clean up the oceans, invent something that solves a big world problem, etc.

STEP 6: WHY

Next, from categories 2 and 4, choose the one goal from each type that is the most inspiring to you, and take a few minutes to write a paragraph about it. Explain why it is so inspiring and why you would want to achieve it. List as many reasons as possible and pick the motivations that drive you most. You are welcome to choose a goal and write a paragraph for each category, but for our purposes, at a minimum, complete the exercise for categories two and four.

*****

Well done. This exercise was meant to get your brain flowing and help you start thinking about what it is you want and do not want out of your life in key areas. This will help you as you focus on a personal vision statement and strategic plan for yourself.

We will next go through a process below that will function as a funnel and enable you to have a clear, crisp, personal vision statement for yourself and one compelling goal at the end of the exercise.

ACTIVITY

YOUR PERSONAL VISION STATEMENT & STRATEGIC PLAN

For my corporate world friends, you know this concept well. Every corporation of any decent size has a vision statement and strategic plan. It usually covers a 3–5-year window, and they use it as a north star to guide their decision-making. It also provides the framework to make annual plans and annual goals.

We need one too in our personal lives. Especially when it comes to your sparkle, you need to have a plan to get it back. You need to write it down so that when life gets chaotic again, and the busyness buries you, you can pull it out and re-inspire your thinking.

You have done a lot of great thinking and reflecting in this book so far, and now we just need to put it into a quick summary format so that you can use it in the next section.

Fill in the worksheet below using the answers you wrote in earlier chapters. You will see references to the chapter so you can quickly grab your answers.

(Worksheet On Following Page)

SUMMARY WORKSHEET

(You will use this in the next section to create your vision and goals. There is a blank template in the Appendix if you need it).

PART 1: YOUR CURRENT STATE SUMMARY		
CHAPTER	**QUESTION TO ANSWER**	**ANSWER(S)** *(Examples Included)*
2	My current burnout score on a scale of 1-10 is:	*10*
5	What my career has gotten me so far:	*Wealth, "Things"*
5	What I *don't* have:	*Happiness, Time*
5	I do (or do not) feel I am getting a good ROI out of the investment I'm making in my workplace.	*I Do <u>Not</u>*
3	The scenario that best describes my current life situation is: (Wall, Whack, Dip, Racetrack, Caution Light)	*I've hit a wall*
14	The 1-2 biggest sparkle stealers I battle against are:	*Side-eyeing and sloppy thoughts*

WHO AM I?		
CHAPTER	**QUESTION TO ANSWER**	**ANSWER(S)**
8	My 1-2 core values are:	*Flexibility and Family*
9	My 1-2 dominant personality colors are:	*Red, Green*
10	My 1-2 greatest superpowers are:	*Awesome at getting tactical things done*
11	I am allergic to:	*Social events*
12	My currency in life is:	*Time*

MY SPARKLE		
CHAPTER ANSWER(S)	**QUESTION**	
13	The 1-2 things that must be true for me to experience joy & meaning in my working life are:	*I must have time and space to do what I want*
13	In this life, I want to bring ___ and _____ to _____.	*Kindness and clarity to the working world*
12	To do that, I must be _____ and _____.	*Bold and authentic*
14	The types of rest I most need to restore my sparkle are _____ and _____.	*Emotional Rest and Creative Rest*
6	Going forward, I will define success in terms of _____ and _____.	*Flexibility and Freedom*

	My "why" is:	*Less Stress, More Meaning*

PART 2: YOUR VISION and GOALS

Use your answers from the worksheet to help you reflect and answer the below questions.

YOUR VISION STATEMENT

Description: What you want to give to the world and to whom you want to give it.

Directions: Complete this sentence. Refer back to the values you wrote down earlier in the book from Chapter 8 and your definition of success from Chapter 6 if it's helpful.

"In this life, I want to bring _____ and _____ to _____. "

Fill in the blanks with 2 or 3 words that feel right deep in your soul.

Example: In this life, I want to bring inspiration, clarity, and kindness to employees in the corporate world.

Yours could be a different set of words and a different audience. Only you know the audience you are meant to serve, and what it is you can bring to them. For example, your audience might be the world, your city, your neighborhood, your workplace, a specific demographic, certain geography, etc.

YOUR SUPERPOWERS

Directions: Complete this sentence. Use the answers from the superpower section in your thinking here.

"I want to use my superpowers of _____ and _____ to bring _____ and _____ to _____.

Example: "I want to use my superpowers of writing and clear thinking to bring inspiration, clarity, and kindness to employees in the corporate world.

YOUR TO-BE LIST

Directions: Complete this sentence with words that describe how you need to be and show up in the world to accomplish that vision.

This will require me to be _____, _____, and _____.

Example: This will require me to be courageous, authentic, and confident.

YOUR IDEAL SCENE

Directions: Use the words from Step 3 to fill in the first three blanks and then fill in the last two blanks.

For the last two blanks, reflect on your personality type and allergies from earlier in the book. Think about the environments where you feel like you are the most in your flow zone and have the most joy.

I am my most _____, _____, and _____ self when I am in a working environment where I can be _____ and _____.

Example: I am my most courageous, authentic, and creative self in a working environment where I can be calm, unhurried, and unscheduled.

YOUR CURRENT SCENE

Directions: Pick either the word does or does not to complete the sentence. If "does" is selected with the caveat that something else must first be true, then list that condition at the end of the sentence.

My current working environment <u>does</u> or <u>does not</u> offer me options to be _____, _____, and _____.

Example: My current working environment does offer me options to be calm, unhurried, and unscheduled if I am in a different department/team/role.

Example: My current working environment does not offer me options to be calm, unhurried, and unscheduled.

WHAT YOU NEED MOST

Directions: Complete this sentence with the one thing you most need to create the environment that will best enable you to achieve your vision. Be as specific as you can.

The one thing I most need to create this environment, which will enable me to achieve my vision, is _____.

Example: The one thing I most need to create this environment is the courage and conviction to leave my job and start my own company.

Other examples of what you may need, depending on your circumstances and the environment you are trying to create:

- A loved one's support for the change.
- A larger financial security blanket, for example, a six-month emergency fund or paying off a specific bill first.
- A manager's support to change jobs, change teams, or try a different career path.
- Support to attend a specific type of training event or conference that will help you get the skills that you need.
- A more flexible schedule.
- Joining a new company or getting a new job doing XYZ.

WHAT YOU ARE WILLING TO GIVE UP

Directions: Complete the sentences.

I am willing to sacrifice _____ to create this environment and achieve my vision.

Example: I am willing to sacrifice my personal need for stability to create this environment and achieve my vision.

I am *not* willing to sacrifice _____.

Example: I am not willing to sacrifice my short-term financial security.

A GUT CHECK

Directions: Complete the sentence.

My conviction level and level of desire in creating this environment and achieving my vision is, on a scale of 1 to 10, a _____ .

Example: My conviction level and level of desire in creating this environment to achieve my vision are, on a scale of 1 to 10, a 12.

THE GOAL

Directions: Complete the sentence with one significant goal you want to achieve next year that will bring you closer to your vision.

By (insert the date that is exactly one year from today) _____ , I will have _____ as a major step forward in achieving my vision.

Example: By Jan 1, 2024, I will have saved enough money to give me at least six months of financial security that will enable me to be able to resign from my job on Feb 1, 2024, and begin the start of my new company.

THE PLAN

Directions: Complete the sentences with a specific action you can take in the specified period. This will start and sustain a wave of momentum toward the direction of your vision and enable you to complete your one-year goal.

In the next 24 hours, I will _____ to create momentum for my vision.

Example: In the next 24 hours, I will write a letter of encouragement to myself to create momentum for my vision. I want to capture the excitement and ideas I have in my head right now, and I will ask my sister to mail them to me in one week.

In the next 90 days, I will _____ to create further momentum for my vision.

In the next 180 days, I will _____ to create further momentum for my vision.

SAMPLE

Here is a sample finished version.

PERSONAL PLAN and VISION (Sample)

MY VISION

In this life, I want to bring inspiration, clarity, and kindness to employees in the corporate world.

THE SUPERPOWERS I WILL USE

I want to use my superpowers of writing and clear thinking to bring inspiration, clarity, and kindness to employees in the corporate world.

MY 'TO-BE' LIST

This will require me to be courageous, authentic, and confident.

MY IDEAL SCENE

I am my most courageous, authentic, and creative self in a working environment where I can be calm, unhurried, and unscheduled.

ASSESSMENT OF MY CURRENT ENVIRONMENT

My current working environment does not offer me calm, unhurried, and unscheduled options.

WHAT I NEED MOST

The one thing I most need to create this environment that will enable me to achieve my vision is the courage and conviction to leave my job and start my own company.

WHAT I AM WILLING TO SACRIFICE

I am willing to sacrifice my personal need for stability to create this environment and achieve my vision.

WHAT I AM NOT WILLING TO SACRIFICE
I am not willing to sacrifice my short-term financial security.

MY CONVICTION LEVEL
My conviction level and level of desire in creating this environment and achieving my vision are, on a scale of 1 to 10, a 12.

MY GOAL AND PLAN
By Jan 1, 2024, I will have saved enough money to give me at least six months of financial security, which will enable me to resign from my job on Feb 1, 2024, and begin the start of my new company.

In the next 24 hours, I will write a letter of encouragement to myself to create momentum for my vision. I want to capture the excitement and ideas I have in my head right now, and I will ask my sister to mail it to me in one week.

In the next 90 days, I will _____. In the next 180 days, I will _____.

MY SENTENCE
Directions: Now, take all that and make yourself an inspiring one-sentence cheat sheet you can stick on your computer. Word it however you want.

My Sentence:

Example: Amy, discipline = freedom for you. Save for the next year and by Feb 1, launch your business! You CAN do this. You WANT to do this. You NEED to do this.

CHAPTER SUMMARY ACTIVITY

****

REFLECTION QUESTIONS

This was an intense section, well done!

Now do a gut check for yourself...how are you feeling? Take some time now to go for a walk and reflect on your thoughts from this chapter. Get outside in nature and do a walk of reflection and meditation to thank yourself for doing the work to get to this point. Whether you feel inspired or overwhelmed, you are still making progress. This amount of reflection is hard work, reward yourself now!

CHAPTER REFLECTION NOTES

_____

_____

_____

_____

_____

_____

_____

_____

CHAPTER APPENDIX: BLANK WORKSHEET

PART 1: YOUR CURRENT STATE SUMMARY		
CHAPTER	**QUESTION TO ANSWER**	**ANSWER (S)** *(Examples Included)*
2	My current burnout score on a scale of 1-10 is:	
4	What my career has gotten me so far:	
4	What I *don't* have:	
4	I do (or do not) feel I am getting a good ROI out of the investment I'm making in my workplace.	
3	The scenario that best describes my current life situation is: (Wall, Whack, Dip, Racetrack, Caution Light)	
13	The 1-2 biggest sparkle stealers I battle against are:	
WHO AM I?		
CHAPTER	**QUESTION TO ANSWER**	**ANSWER (S)**
7	My 1-2 core values are:	
8	My 1-2 dominant personality colors are:	
9	My 1-2 greatest superpowers are:	

10	I am allergic to:	
11	My currency in life is:	
	MY SPARKLE	
12	The 1-2 things that must be true for me to experience joy & meaning in my working life are:	
12	In this life, I want to bring ___ and _____ to _____.	
12	To do that, I must be _____ and _____.	
15	The types of rest I most need to restore my sparkle are _____ and _____.	
5	Going forward, I will define success in terms of _____ and _____.	

REFLECTIONS

CHAPTER 19

ROLE MODELS and REAL-LIFE SPARKLERS

Many brave souls I have met along the way of my sparkle journey proved to me that these inspirational quotes, pithy one-liners, brain-bending thinking questions, and tough love kicks in the pants do work. They have shown me that real change and true transformation are possible. They have shown me that taking control of the joy in your life is possible.

Here are a few examples so you can see what this all looks like in real life, and that there is a possibility. There are many paths and ways to create the sparkle in your life, even in the most restrictive of circumstances and these stories prove it.

SPARKLE STORIES

Creative Schedules & Volunteering

Mary was a single mom of two children who found herself in a job that gave her little joy. She had always been good at math and had wanted to be a high school math teacher. Still, life had other plans for her, and she had her first child at an early age and could not finish her education. So, she ended up taking a job as a bookkeeper at a local hardware store, thinking, "well, at least I'll be around numbers."

She found that she was working in the backroom of the store, in a windowless room with little interaction with others, and was stuck staring at spreadsheets all day. She was good at it, and it came easily to her, but she felt an increasing sense that there had to be more to life for her, and she craved a chance to make a difference in the life of children.

Her child's school had sent a note asking if anyone would like to be an after-school math tutor a couple of days a week.

Mary immediately felt a strong pull towards this opportunity and wanted to raise her hand. There are only so many hours in a day though, and she had yet to learn how she would find the time to do the tutoring, her full-time job, and raising her two kids.

She was determined to figure it out, so she went to her boss, explained the situation, and asked him if she could leave early twice a week to do the tutoring. She committed that there would be no lapse in her duties, and she asked if he would be open to a two-week trial period. Mary was a valued employee, and her boss didn't want to lose her, so he was much more flexible than she anticipated and agreed to the trial.

The trial went as planned. She was able to manage her schedule at work and do tutoring a couple of days a week. She found that her heart was much fuller at the end of the week, and she found a renewed sense of joy in her life.

Making a Secure Leap

Tanya loved to bake and had dreams of one day opening a bakery but could not imagine how she could ever find the time or the financial resources to even consider it. She had a full-time corporate job in marketing that kept her busy, and she had a limited emergency fund. One day, she attended a leadership training class at work. It involved a team-building exercise where everyone shared a dream they had accomplished.

Tanya was inspired by the stories she heard and humbled by the support she got from her peers when she spoke of wanting to open her own bakery (her peers all knew how good her cookies were!). She decided that she was determined to make this a reality. She committed to reducing some of her optional expenses and building up a six-month emergency fund that she could use to one day test out her bakery idea.

While she was building up her financial safety blanket, she also began experimenting with new recipes, started to bake a couple of evenings a week, and sold her cookies at the local farmers market on the weekend. Very quickly, word spread in her small town about her delicious goodies, and she found herself with more orders than she could keep up with. She was working many evenings during the week now and could build up her financial fund much faster than she thought she could.

So, at the end of six months, she decided to take the leap and resigned from her job to do her baking full-time. As it happened, a local baker was selling his bakery and she bought it. In addition, her marketing skills came in very handy in getting the word out about her business.

Within a year of opening the business, she was making more from the business than she had in her old job. She felt a tremendous sense of joy and excitement every day.

Career Switch

Antoine was an up-and-coming high potential in the corporate finance world and had worked his way up into a successive series of roles that gave him increasing responsibility. He had everything he thought he wanted. He had a great job, a great car, a great salary, and he was at a great company, but the more he advanced, the more he realized that he was allergic to a large portion of his job. He reflected on his career path and realized that because he had always been good at math, his parents suggested he major in business and finance in college, so he did.

After college, he joined a well-known corporation, and his parents were thrilled. He had job security and a great career path ahead of him. What he really wanted though, was to become a chef, but he shelved that dream away for another day.

About two years in, he started to feel a tug that this was not his career path, but he was too afraid to leave such a great gig and did not want to disappoint his parents, so he stayed on the path.

Around the age of forty, Antoine had a serious medical condition arise that his doctors attributed to the stress of his job. He had experienced a whack and was staring directly into a wall. He knew he had to make a change. He started to think about his younger self and his dreams of becoming a chef, and he could feel his energy rise. Tom began to explore options at a local cooking school and discovered that he could attend portions of culinary school on the weekends.

He didn't know if he would have the time, but he knew he had to try. So, he gave himself six months to test it out and see if the dream of becoming a chef was still there. What he found was not only was it there, but it was growing.

So, after a year had gone by, he decided to resign from his position and went into culinary school full-time. He later became head chef at a local restaurant, and you could almost taste the sparkle in his food.

****

These are just a few stories. There are many more. There are stories of people who created "hyphen-careers," where they had a full-time day job but found creative ways to create space that allowed them to be something else. For example, I have a friend that says he is an HR manager/BBQ master.

Others found creative ways to stay in their current job but slowly transitioned into another job that gave them more joy. Others were able to maneuver their finances or schedules to take a leap of faith and start their own business. Others were able to take their current job, talk to their manager, and create new job descriptions that still met the organization's needs but also allowed them to do work that put them more into their flow zone.

Here is a brief list of ways others have reclaimed their sparkle:

TANGIBLE WAYS TO RECLAIM YOUR SPARKLE

Same Company, Same Job, Different Team

If you love the actual work of your job and the company, but not the team, you could consider looking for another job in the company, in the same job, but in a different team. Admittedly, this only works if you work for a large corporation with multiple teams doing the same work.

Also, before you make this move, take a hard look in the mirror, and ensure you haven't fallen into some of our rut stories that we talked about before. The old saying, "wherever you go, there you are" will apply in this scenario. Make sure it's not you that you need to work on versus your team members.

Same Company, New Job

Many can reclaim their spark by better aligning their superpower to a different job within their current company. This could involve a new role in a current team or another team within the same company.

Many corporations offer tuition reimbursement that can help in this scenario. You can attend various external training options that will give you a skillset in a new area while you are still in your current job. This will help you be more competitive as you apply and compete for new jobs in your company.

Shift to Part-Time

Some find their sparkle in something outside of work, and their biggest desire is more time and flexibility. Many people were able to work out part-time roles or even job-sharing arrangements that allowed them more freedom and flexibility in their personal lives. This creates opportunities, for example, for hyphen-careers as I described earlier (ex., accountant-jeweler, nurse-writer).

Job Description Modification or Addition

You may not realize this is an option, but I have seen it happen a few different times. If most of your job does not give you energy, think about the components that do. If there is one that you have a particular passion or superpower in, consider asking your manager if you can do more of that in exchange for less of something else.

You may even volunteer to take on extra project work for the team in that specific area. As a result, you may be able to trade off some duties with others in the team. You would be surprised at how much flexibility there might be if you approach your manager professionally, proactively, and creatively to make the 'and' equation work. Figure out the intersection between what they want and what you want.

New Company

Some find that the job was right, but the culture did not fit them. They were able to find a renewed sense of energy and creativity doing the same kind of job but in a different environment and a different company. A friendly word of advice on this one though. If possible, secure your new job before you leave your current job. It is easier to find a new job when you have a job. That said, don't stress if you can't stay in your current job. It may give you more time to do the networking that you'll need to do to find that new role.

Same Field, Different Type of Role

You may love your line of work and the field you are in but find that the demands of your specific job are more than you can give in this season of your life. In those instances, there may be other options in your field. For example, if you are a nurse and love caring for others, but the long hours and never-ending patient load are taking their toll, you could transition to roles like home-health nursing, nurse education, or nurse case management. Before making a switch, though, identify what exactly it is you are solving for (ex., more flexibility, more time with patients, less admin, etc.).

Career Track Shift

Some people realize that while they like the company they work for, their sparkle is in an entirely different career path. They then make a series of decisions that will enable them to pursue that new path. For example, you could speak with your manager or Human Resources department to put together an individual development plan and a long-term career path that will enable you to switch to a different field.

You may have to take a step backward or into a more junior role at first, but often you can make a lateral move into a different field. Ways to prepare for this include getting certification and training in your new field, volunteering to do a project in a team in that new area, shadowing employees that work in that team, or finding an on-ramp role. On-ramp roles are those roles that have more general experience requirements in that field and don't require a large number of years of experience or a specialized skill within the field (disclaimer – many of the on-ramp roles may be more junior).

For example, many IT roles now do not require degrees. Instead, you can take an external certification proving you have the skill and knowledge in that area. You can pursue these certifications on your own time to help smooth the path to the field. In addition, your company's tuition reimbursement program may be able to help fund the cost.

Complete Career Shift

Some, like me, realized that they are in the wrong career field and needed to make more of a drastic change. This could include leaving the field and leaving the company. Most people plan for this at least 6 to 12 months ahead of time to minimize the downside risk. For example, you might need to cut your expenses and save more to build up a financial nest egg that will allow you to quit and open your own business. Many people take advantage of the side hustle culture and start their new life on the weekends and evenings. For example, if you want to be a writer, you can start writing in the evenings. If you want to bake, you can bake as you have time. Building up some portion of your business on the side is a good idea so that you aren't starting cold after you resign your position.

Quitting and Start Your Own Business

For the blues in the audience with ideas that sparkle in their brain 24/7, going off into the entrepreneurial world and trying your ideas may be exactly what you need. You also know you will never be happy until you try. If you are leaving a great company or career behind, you can always come back if you leave on good terms. Many people find their sparkle via this path. Don't be afraid of this path and don't be afraid of being seen as a quitter. Just because you are quitting your corporate role, does not mean you are quitting work. As Seth Godin says in *The Dip*, "quitting a job is not quitting your quest to make a living or difference or an impact. A job is just a tactic, a way to get what you really want. As soon as your job hits a dead end, it makes sense to quit and take your quest to a bigger marketplace - because every day you wait puts your goal further away." [91]

Recruit a New Tribe

Motivational speaker Jim Rohn once said, "You are the average of the five people you spend the most time with."[92] Consider that for yourself. Are the people you spend the most time with optimistic? Do they come from a place of abundance versus scarcity? Do they champion, encourage, and speak the truth to you? Do they give you a sense of energy and joy when you are around them? Or does your circle keep you stuck in some of your rut stories? If so, you may need to recruit some new people to be a part of your life and re-evaluate the amount of time you spend with some people in your circle.

Volunteering

Volunteering could be a way to find new people for your tribe. Some people find great meaning and purpose in volunteering in their community or elsewhere. Given there are only so many hours in the day, you may need to take a hard look at how and where you spend your time and make tradeoffs to allow yourself to spend time doing activities that give you more energy.

Time Away

Sometimes, you just have to call a time out. Maybe it's an extended vacation. Maybe it's a sabbatical, or maybe as my friend said, you just need an intermission. Sometimes this is just what the doctor ordered. This will allow you to reset and restore. This is likely easier said than done though, as financial or family obligations may pull you in a different direction. Just remember you cannot give what you don't have, and this time away may very well be the best investment you ever make in yourself.

Take Care of Yourself

A lack of physical fitness and eating healthy may silently rob you of your sparkle. The fatigue and brain fog that creeps into your day can prevent you from feeling at your best (or even just average). Consulting your doctor, a nutritionist, or a fitness trainer to consider how to incorporate this back into your life could provide long-lasting benefits.

*****

The possibilities are endless. Don't let fear or scarcity thinking rob you of an opportunity to find your sparkle again. Be courageous and be creative in pursuing options that will improve your working life. You may believe that career doors and possibilities closed for you long ago, but they haven't. It just takes a gentle nudge (ok maybe a hard push sometimes too!) to open the door back up. You don't have to wander, and you don't have to wonder any longer. Take ownership of your life and your options. You can do this.

CHAPTER SUMMARY ACTIVITY

****

REFLECTION QUESTIONS

- Who is a real-life 'sparkler' that you know?
- What is their story?
- What obstacle did they have to overcome?
- How did they do it?
- What can you learn from them?

CHAPTER REFLECTION NOTES

_____

_____

_____

_____

_____

_____

_____

_____

_____

CHAPTER 20

IT IS TIME

Henry David Thoreau once said, "Things do not change. We change."

If you have read this far in this book, first, thank you. Thank you for letting me into your life and your busy schedule. Thank you for allowing the conversation in your head to go where it needed to go. Thank you for being honest and vulnerable with yourself. Thank you for asking yourself the tough questions and taking a good long look at yourself in the mirror.

This kind of work is not easy, but it can be life-changing. It can be transformative. It can be joyous.

As Albert Einstein once said, the definition of insanity is doing the same thing over and over and expecting a different result. I know I was caught in an endless cycle of repeating hollow successes, repeating mistakes, repeating frustrations, and repeating excuses. I thought that's just how life was designed to be. It wasn't until I had two whacks and slammed into a 10-foot wall, that life got my attention, sat me down at the kitchen table, and had a long hard talk with me.

It wasn't until months after I made some hard decisions and put in the time to reflect and plan that I started to realize an entirely different life was possible for me. It had been right in front of me the whole time. If you feel trapped, paralyzed, frozen in place or are in any of the "It is Time" scenarios we talked through, your time is *now*.

Please don't wait for all the chips to fall in place or for all the stoplights to turn green at the same time. They never will. As I write this final chapter, we are a few days away from New Year's, and resolutions are on my mind. New years are for new beginnings and while many of us have good intentions to change, very few actually do.

Don't be like the 92% of American's who decide to make a change at New Year's and then either never start or quit early. Be in the 8%. [i] If you have read this far, then you know there is something in your life you need to transform. You know deep in your soul that there is more for you my friend and it's time for you to "get off the x" as they say in the military.

The work of transformation and change is not easy. Just ask anyone who has gone through a remodel of their home. There is loud noise, construction dust in every crook and cranny of your home, unrecognizable parts of your home interior for weeks at a time, exposed wiring, trip hazards, and strangers coming in and out of your home constantly. You wonder from five minutes after they start to five minutes before they are done, why you started this process, and you swear that you will never do it again.

But the outcome...the new sparkly kitchen counter, the fancy new bathtub, the bright open space where the dark dingy wall used to be, all give you a feeling of accomplishment and happiness every time you walk in the door.

You have come this far and cracked open your door. Now let yourself walk through it. Just as butterflies must push against their cocoon and go through a messy transformation, so might you. Let yourself be opened up and exposed, let yourself be transformed, and let the light into the deep crevices of your soul, heart, and mind so that you can shine bright for all the world to see.

There is so much beauty inside of you waiting to come out. There is so much energy, flow, and sparkle that the world is eager to see. It is time to start playing offense in your life. It is time to claim the goodness that life wants to give you. There is a universe of possibility in front of you and a moving van packed full of tough hard-won lessons learned, experiences, accomplishments, dreams, goals, and regrets that are ready to drive with you into your new future.

You can decide which boxes you need to unpack when you get there, which ones need to stay boxed up on the shelf, and which ones need to go to the Goodwill. The important part is to get in the driver's seat, plug in your destination, and press the gas.

As Dr. Dalton-Smith describes in her book *Sacred Rest,*

> *"The journey did not take me past rainbows and sunsets. The road was more roller coaster than carousel, more tugboat than luxury cruise liner. There was no fanfare, no celebration along the way. No one cheered to congratulate me for the journey. The course did not move me along like a raft drifting down the calm waters of a country stream. Rather the journey was more like a series of rapids, with leaps from healing bridge to healing bridge."* [93]

This journey is for you and you alone, and while it may not be easy, it will be worth it. As poet Mary Oliver once said, "we all have one wild and precious life to live." You are the one that has to decide what you will do with it. Your reward is in the doing, and in the transformation. Your reward is in the confidence, joy, and sparkle that will rise from deep inside you and light your world.

Show us the way, my friend. Go shine like the 5-carat pink diamond you are, and as Harry Winston once said,

> *"People will stare, so make it worth their while."*

****

The End ♡

APPENDIX

I Would LOVE Your Feedback

Thank you for reading The Sparkle. I would love to hear from you, I believe feedback is a true gift.

If you loved it, hated it or anything in between, I would be grateful for your honest review of the book.

Just head online to wherever you purchased The Sparkle to leave your review.

Even just a quick 1-2 sentences are helpful, and I promise to read every word.

Thank you,

~Robin

Free *Bonus Content* Available!

Congratulations on taking a major step forward in your quest to beat burnout and find your sparkle.

Now, keep your momentum going!!

I would love to walk beside you and have you join our powerful community of sparkle seekers, who just like you, are starting on this exhilarating journey.

Scan the QR code below to join our free community. Receive exclusive access to our weekly newsletter and an entire bonus chapter on how to audit your current environment or the culture of any future prospective employer.

You'll learn all the inside tips on how to assess if a company's culture is right for you and if it will be a sparkle stealer or sparkle giver for you. It is powerful knowledge to have.

I'll see you inside,

~Robin

Scan to access your free content!

APPENDIX A

CORE VALUES OPTIONS

(Feel free to add your own)

Expression	Trustworthy	Beauty	Passion
Love	Flexible	Balance	Power
Honesty	Caring	Clarity	Spirituality
Curiosity	Gratefulness	Community	Resilience
Focus	Openness	Diversity	Romance
Skillfulness	Compassion	Integrity	Security
Industrious	Courage	Expertise	Stability
Protective	Friendliness	Fitness	Expressive
Respectful	Forgiveness	Freedom	Service
Acceptance	Independence	Generosity	Teamwork
Creativity	Playfulness	Grit	Rest
Helpfulness	Authenticity	Growth	Wisdom
Mindfulness	Supportive	Health	Vitality
Joyfulness	Kindness	Humor	Commitment
Assertiveness	Success	Intelligence	Loyalty
Orderliness	Athleticism	Intimacy	Nature

APPENDIX B

DEEPER DIVE ON SPIRITUAL REST

In full transparency, I have struggled to write this section more than any other part of this book. I have written and rewritten this section at least three times, it's 9:30 p.m., and my brain is tired, but my spirit is strong.

I have a battle raging within me between the classically trained HR professional I have been for 20 years and the deeply flawed yet greatly loved follower of Jesus Christ that I have also been for those 20 years.

The HR professional in me intellectually believes that what I want to say on this topic may not seem inclusive or politically correct enough because it would focus on one specific type of spirituality and not others.

I have done my best thus far in the book to walk a fine line and to sprinkle my faith in places that felt natural. And then this section comes along and throws me right off my tightrope. This same battle was one of my personal sparkle stealers in my job as an HR leader because I always felt a need to temper the sharing of my faith.

You can imagine all the situations I became involved in that dealt with personal and human challenges. The name of the function, after all, is Human Resources. Many times, I felt like I had the answer that the troubled person in my office desperately needed to hear. Still, I kept silent and gave a vanilla, more generic yet corporately acceptable answer. I felt a deep sadness, frustration, and regret each time.

So, when I spoke earlier about authenticity and acting one way when you feel another, I lived that on a deeply personal level every single day at work. I am not the in-your-face, Bible-thumping, high-horse, judgmental, fire-and-brimstone-breathing kind of Christian that I believe too many have experienced in recent years. I believe that repels people away from God.

I am much more of a heart-thumping, Bible-reading, practically minded, love and kindness-breathing kind of Christian who also is not afraid to shoot you straight.

I love you too much, dear friend, not to share what I and billions around the world believe to be the greatest source of comfort, healing, joy, peace, and rest that will ever be possible in this chaotic and increasingly fear-inducing world, especially when the chapter topic is one centered on spiritual rest.

So, if talk of spiritual things and Christianity makes you itchy, this is your chance to skip this section, but I strongly believe you will be missing out on the most significant source in the universe of sparkle. Nothing I have said in this book thus far will hold a candle to the power of this source.

Here are some Bible verses (there are many more) that talk about the rest we have in God that I find comforting:

"Come to me, all you who are weary and burdened, and I will give you rest. Take my yoke upon you and learn from me, for I am gentle and humble in heart, and you will find rest for your souls." ~Matthew 11:28-29 [94]

"And the peace of God, which transcends all understanding, will guard your hearts and your minds in Christ Jesus." ~Philippians 4:7 [95]

The Lord replied, "My Presence will go with you, and I will give you rest." ~Exodus 33:14 [96]

"The Lord is my shepherd; I lack nothing. He makes me lie down in green pastures, he leads me beside quiet waters, He refreshes my soul. He

guides me along the right paths for his name's sake. Even though I walk through the darkest valley, I will fear no evil, for you are with me; your rod and your staff, they comfort me. You prepare a table before me in the presence of my enemies. You anoint my head with oil; my cup overflows. Surely your goodness and love will follow me all the days of my life, and I will dwell in the house of the Lord forever. ~Psalms 23 [97]

"I have told you these things, so that in me you may have peace. In this world, you will have trouble. But take heart! I have overcome the world." ~John 16:33 [98]

Spiritual Rest Deficit Symptoms:

Feelings of discouragement, weariness, emptiness, and overall lack of meaning and fulfillment. A sense that something is missing in your life that you haven't been able to fill. Feelings of fear and panic at the thought of serious sickness and death.

Description:

We have talked a lot about questions in this book, but the biggest and most important questions you will ever ask yourself, whether you are 18 or 80 years old, are:

1. Do I believe in God?

2. Do I trust him with my life and to save me from my sin?

3. Do I accept his offer to save me, and will I let him be Lord of my life?

(That all sounds churchy, I know, and the all-business, practical, keep-it-light side of me is trying to find a better way to say it, so bear with me for now).

There are just three things I want you to know about God and his rest:

1. God is real and is right here.
2. God is love.
3. God is rest.

God is real. History proves it. Science proves it. Creation proves it. I won't over-index on this one because you can and should search the Internet and your hearts for evidence if you need it, but I will give you a book to read if it's helpful. It's called *The Case for Christ* by Lee Strobel. [99]

It was written by an atheist who was an investigative journalist who set out to prove God wasn't real and instead ended up completely believing in God. The book digs deep into what he finds. I can also tell you from personal experience he is real. I have many powerful examples in my life where I have felt God's presence and seen his work in person. For example, when I accepted Jesus's offer to save me, while it didn't happen overnight, I became much less anxious because I no longer worry about dying. I can't wait to get to Heaven. It is so much better than this broken and chaotic world. I have a peace I can't describe and wouldn't trade it for any amount of money.

If you ever want a view of what Heaven is like, I highly recommend the book *Imagine Heaven* by John Burke. It is one of the most powerful books I have ever read and makes Jesus so much more real. I used to think of Heaven as this abstract, 24/7 church service, which didn't have a lot of appeal to me. Heaven is so much better than that. It is a real physical place, full of pure joy, pure love, and pure peace. It is full of art, music, things to do, and activities that fill your soul. There is no sickness, no dying, no tears, no sin, and no evil. It is full of people you love who went to Heaven and most importantly, it is where Jesus is.

Jesus is the purest form of love, grace, mercy, peace, patience, kindness, and gentleness in the universe. He knows us inside and out, to the deepest level, and loves us despite knowing all the sins we've committed, and all of our flaws.

I want to be with Jesus with every fiber of my being, and I am fascinated by Heaven. Did you know over 9 million people in the U.S.

have had a near-death experience, and all have had nearly the same experiences and glimpses of Heaven? [100] These are people from all over the world, all different religions, atheists, doctors, lawyers, all different races. They all had nearly the same exact experience, it's incredible actually.

Here are some excerpts from *Imagine Heaven* that I love. These are from people who had NDE experiences, visited Heaven briefly, and came back.

"I saw colors I would never have believed existed. I've never felt more alive than I did then. I was home. I was where I belonged. I wanted to be there more than I had ever wanted to be anywhere on Earth. Here on Earth, we don't ever feel fully known, understood, or valued by others or even ourselves. In Heaven, this all gets replaced with an unbelievable clarity of who God created you to be – fully yourself, fully unique, for a unique relationship with your Creator."

"I felt totally exposed and transparent before God. You can wear masks with other people but not with God. I felt ashamed and undone...but a wave of pure unconditional love flowed over me to my amazement. It was the last thing I expected. Instead of judgment, I was being washed with pure love. Pure, unadulterated, clean, uninhibited, undeserved love. It began to fill me from the inside out. I found myself beginning to weep uncontrollably as the love became stronger and stronger. This love was healing my heart, and I began to understand there is incredible hope for mankind in this love."

"I felt like I could get lost in his eyes. In his eyes, I saw the love for every human and creation of God. When he looked at me, his eyes pierced me all the way through. It was pure love. I melted in his presence. Jesus' eyes were deep, beautiful pools of love." [101]

(Side note – there is a young girl, now in her twenties, that had a profound experience with God as a child and has been a child prodigy in art ever since. She has painted many images of God and you can see the paintings on her website, https://akiane.com. People that have had NDEs say the photo she made of Jesus is the closest they have ever seen to what he looks like.)

God's Masterpiece

God created you. You are his masterpiece, his one-of-a-kind work of art. Unfortunately, we are all also damaged masterpieces in need of restoration. Sin infected humanity when Eve bit the forbidden fruit. Now we all have sin in us every day.

Because of our sin, no one can be with God in Heaven who has not been first washed and forgiven of their sin. And we all sin. If you've ever told the whitest of lies, gotten angry, been jealous, been judgmental, unforgiving, or a dozen other sins, then you are guilty.

And because God is a just God, the sins have to be punished, and that punishment is to be eternally separated from him in hell. Hell is the vilest and evilest of places. It's full of darkness, extreme pain, and extreme loneliness.

BUT the good news is that God gave us a way out. God sent his only son, whose name is Jesus Christ, to come to this evil crazy place called Earth and to save us. He lived here for 30 years as a full human being. He performed all kinds of miracles, showed extreme counter-culture love, and shared what God is all about which is pure love. He did this all to save us from ourselves. Jesus wasn't just born in a manger, he has existed with God since the beginning of time, and the manger was just him coming down to earth in a form we could relate to.

For us not to go to hell and not to be forever separated from God, Jesus volunteered for one of the toughest jobs around. He volunteered to come to Earth and pay the price for the sins of me, you, and our 117 billion (and counting) friends, who have lived on this Earth for the last

192,000 years. How did he do that? How much would that kind of sin debt cost? A lot.

It's a debt we can never work our way out of. It doesn't matter how many good works we do in our life; it will never fully pay the price. The only way it could happen was for Jesus to pay it for us, and it cost him his life via a brutally cruel death, and he volunteered for the job.

Jesus died the cruelest form of death humanity has ever devised, crucifixion. I won't go into much detail about that process, but you can research it and find out just how awful it was. And the physical pain wasn't even the worst of it. Jesus was utterly alone and shut out from his father for the entire time he hung on the cross. God was completely silent and turned his face from him. To be a just God, God had to let his son take on the full wrath of his judgment in our place.

That cruel death, that separation from God, is what *we* deserved, not Jesus. Jesus never sinned one time yet took the penalty for us.

After Jesus died, the greatest news that will ever be on Earth was that he was buried for three days and then rose from the dead and walked on the Earth (yes, literally walked again) for 40 days. Over five hundred people physically saw him and spoke to him.

And on the 40th day, Jesus ascended into Heaven in front of his eleven disciples. If Jesus had not risen from the dead, then Christianity is worthless. It is what separates Christianity from all other religions, it is why we celebrate Easter, and it means that because Jesus lives again, we get to do the same thing after we die. We also keep living.

God has given us an incredible gift, but it doesn't mean we automatically get it. Heaven is not our default destination; we have to do a few things first:

What To Do:
 1 – Believe in him, that he is real and that he sent his son to Earth to die for us.

 2 – Tell him you are sorry for the sins you have committed (and mean it) and ask for him to forgive you.

 3 – Ask him to save you and be your God and best friend.

If it's helpful, here is a prayer you can pray (or put into your own words):

"Dear God, I know that I am a sinner and I am so sorry. I want to turn away from my sin. I believe Jesus Christ is your Son; I believe he died on the cross for my sin and that you raised him from the dead. I want him to come into my heart and take control of my life. I trust him with my heart and life and want to follow him as Lord from this day forward. In Jesus' name. Amen."

✳✳✳✳✳✳

That's it. Once we do those things, we are forever saved, and no one can take it away from us.

Once you've prayed that prayer, God will send his Holy Spirit to live in your heart and to give you guidance and strength. Use the Holy Spirit's help to turn from your sins and day by day stop them as best you can.

Your life will start to change. It may happen little by little or in a radical transformation like the Apostle Paul. Either way, you'll crave learning more about God, you'll pray, you'll wonder why everyone doesn't accept him, and you'll want to tell others about him.

If you aren't quite there yet, I have two recommendations:

Read the Bible. The Bible is God's love letter and instruction manual to us and will tell you everything you need to know. I would encourage you to get a Bible and read the book of Genesis and the book of John as a starting point. Keep reading the New Testament until you finish. Every chapter in the New Testament is full of God's love and guidance to us.

Watch the TV series, *The Chosen*. This may seem like an odd recommendation, but this is one of the most powerful shows I have ever seen, and it brings Jesus to life in an incredible way. It's completely free to watch. If you have a smart TV, you can watch it on Amazon™, Netflix™, or YouTube™. You can also download their app and watch it on your phone, and cast it to your TV from the app. They also have DVDs that you can buy. I am also happy to send you a copy for free if you need it.

If you are still skeptical, great, that at least means your brain is thinking about it, and it's the Holy Spirit talking to you. I encourage you to do your homework. You won't be able to hide from the answers. If you have accepted him, hallelujah, find a church to plug into and talk to. I promise there are good, loving, and kind churches out there.

If you are sitting on the fence, that's okay too. Just don't sit too long. Life is short and unexpected, and none of us knows if we have one more minute left to ponder the most important question in the world.

If you have more questions and want to talk to someone, I would recommend contacting the Billy Graham organization. They have a free, confidential and non-judgmental set of Christian volunteers who are available 24/7 online and via phone. Here are ways to contact them:

- Toll free, 24/7 Phone Line – For prayer requests or questions – 1-888-388-2683.
- Online at peacewithGod.net. For Spanish, visit PazConDios.net
- If you would like a personal coach to guide you in your new walk with God, you can contact them at KnowJesus.net or ConociendoaJesus.net for Spanish.
- Email: help@bgea.org
- Free weekly email devotional – billygraham.org/subscriptions

****

If I had only two words to end this section, I would say, "Look Up." Look up to the heavens to God for the peace and rest you so desperately seek. Look up and see the face of Jesus Christ and see the nail scars on his hands to experience the purest, most overwhelming love you have ever known. Look up when your soul feels empty, your mind is weary, and your heart is broken.

Look up when fear and anxiety are crashing over you, look up when you feel like there is no safe place to hide in this world, and look up when the storms of suffering and depression feel like they will drown you. Look up when you feel like you have nothing left to give and are at the end of yourself.

Look up when you are paralyzed with fear or confusion and are seeking clarity for your life. Look up when you are desperately searching for your purpose in these short 80-ish years we are on this Earth.

Look up when no medical doctor, therapist, lover, or friend can bring you comfort or fill that cross-shaped hole in your heart. Look up when all the best science and technology in the world cannot heal the most important person in the world to you. Look up when the fear of death is staring you in the face so intently that you can't breathe. *Look Up.*

We started this section with three questions, and I hope your answer will be yes. God is so in love with you. He has been chasing you all your life. Let him catch you. Fall into his arms of love and rest. It is time.

~John 3:16

****

ACKNOWLEDGEMENTS

This book is the culmination of two decades of working with some of the most incredible people on the planet who have inspired me with their stories of burnout and recovery. It is the result of the generosity of peers and managers who have poured into me with their honesty, grace, time, wisdom, and encouragement.

Thank you to everyone who has given me an encouraging word, a much-needed piece of feedback, a moment of seasoned advice, or their valuable trust. Thank you to the brave men and women who have shared their courageous stories with me. You made this journey possible.

Chris, your support, love, and belief in me have made this chapter of my life and this book possible. Thank you for taking this leap of faith with me. I love you and am so grateful to have you in my life.

Mom, you have been a bright and shining sparkle to me and so many others your whole life. Thank you for being such a role model of love and kindness, I love you.

Sandy, your encouragement and incredible advice have been life-changing. You are one of the most generous and insightful people I know, and I am honored to call you a friend. Thank you for your inspiration, your friendship, and for giving me a push just when I needed it most.

Adam, you have been an incredible champion, friend, and source of constant trust and confidence for me. You have served in many of the roles I talk about in this book and any success I have had in my career is in no small part due to you. Thank you for your wisdom and constant faith in me. It makes a difference.

To Carol, Jenny, Chris, Spencer, Ryan, and Blair, thank you for being a dream team of coworkers and a major source of sparkle for me in a very difficult time. I am forever grateful for your friendship and the fun times we had in the midst of what was hopefully a once-in-a-career experience :--) #Shinebrightlikeadiamond

To April, thank you for being an amazing friend and for your listening ear, encouraging words, and support. To Darlene, thank you for sending me a late-night message of support just when I needed it most, it was a big catalyst for me to start this book.

To my readers, thank you for taking a chance on me. You matter to me.

ABOUT THE AUTHOR

Robin Kirby is an accomplished senior executive within the field of Human Resources. She has spent 25 years at leading Fortune 100 organizations creating cultures that give energy and joy to their employees. Robin has served across the function of HR, including as Chief Human Resources Officer. This gave her a tremendous opportunity to impact the lives of employees at organizations such as General Electric, Citigroup, Honda, Symantec, Infosys, USAA, and Benefitfocus.

She has spent her entire career teaching and learning The Sparkle's principles and is passionate about helping others find their passion and sparkle in life. Robin has lived every word of this book. At the height of her career, she made a conscious decision to step off her corporate career path to pursue a life of more joy and meaning and has never looked back.

She is now an author, blogger, speaker, coach, and consultant to individuals and organizations worldwide and an all-around happier person to be around.

****

If you would like to engage Robin to help you find and reclaim your sparkle through coaching, you can contact her at robinkirby2022@gmail.com. If you are an organization and would like to invite Robin to speak at your next event or consult with you on how to create a sparkle-giving culture, you can also contact her at the email address above.

RESOURCES

[1] Stress and Quality of Working Life: Current Perspectives in Occupational Health, Vol. 37, IAP (2006), pp. 42-49

[2] J. Soc. Issues, 30 (1) (1974), pp. 159-165, 10.1111/j 1540-4560.1974.tb00706.x

[3] World Health Organization, "Burn-out an "occupational phenomenon: International Classification of Diseases," accessed Oct 4, 2022, https://www.who.int/news/item/28-05-2019-burn-out-an-occupational-phenomenon-international-classification-of-diseases

[4] Deloitte, "Workplace Burnout Survey," accessed Oct 7, 2022, https://www2.deloitte.com/us/en/pages/about-deloitte/articles/burnout-survey.html

[5] Achor, Shawn. "9 Out of 10 People Are Willing to Earn Less Money to Do More-Meaningful Work." Harvard Business Review. November 6, 2018. https://hbr.org/2018/11/9-out-of-10-people-are-willing-to-earn-less-money-to-do-more-meaningful-work

[6] Achor, Shawn. "9 Out of 10 People Are Willing to Earn Less Money to Do More-Meaningful Work." Harvard Business Review. November 6, 2018. https://hbr.org/2018/11/9-out-of-10-people-are-willing-to-earn-less-money-to-do-more-meaningful-work

[7] Deloitte, "Workplace Burnout Survey," accessed Oct 7, 2022, https://www2.deloitte.com/us/en/pages/about-deloitte/articles/burnout-survey.html

[8] Wishbae, "Burnout Quotes and Captions for Instagram," accessed October 8, 2022, https://www.wishbae.com/burnout-quotes/

[9] The Mayo Clinic, "How to Spot It and Take Action," Accessed October 15, 2022. https://www.mayoclinic.org/healthy-lifestyle/adult-health/in-depth/burnout/art-20046642

[10] Integris Health, "What are the 5 Stages of Burnout," November 5, 2021, https://integrisok.com/resources/on-your-health/2021/november/what-are-the-5-stages-of-burnout

[11] Integris Health, "What are the 5 Stages of Burnout," November 5, 2021, https://integrisok.com/resources/on-your-health/2021/november/what-are-the-5-stages-of-burnout

[12] Overton, Jenni. "Employee Burnout Statistics for 2022." Limeaid. Accessed September 28, 2022. https://www.limeade.com/resources/blog/employee-burnout-statistics-for-2022/

[13] Setiya, Keiran. "Facing Your Mid-Career Crisis." Harvard Business Review. March 2019. https://hbr.org/2019/03/facing-your-mid-career-crisis

[14] Setiya, Keiran. "Facing Your Mid-Career Crisis." Harvard Business Review. March 2019. https://hbr.org/2019/03/facing-your-mid-career-crisis

[15] Smith, Morgan. "Teachers are in the Midst of a Burnout Crisis." MSNBC. Accessed Dec 1, 2022. https://www.cnbc.com/2022/11/22/teachers-are-in-the-midst-of-a-burnout-crisis-it-became-intolerable.html#:~:text=K%2D12%20teachers%20report%20the,a%20June%202022%20Gallup%20poll.

[16] United States Department of Health and Human Services, "New Surgeon General Advisory Sounds Alarm on Health Worker Burnout and Resignation," May 23, 2022, https://www.hhs.gov/about/news/2022/05/23/new-surgeon-general-advisory-sounds-alarm-on-health-worker-burnout-and-resignation.html

[17] Dalton-Smith, Dr. Saundra, *Sacred Rest: Recover Your Life, Renew Your Energy, Restore Your Sanity* (Tennessee: FaithWords, 2017)

[18] Petersen, Anne Helen, "How Millennials Became the Burnout Generation." BuzzFeed, January 5, 2019. https://www.buzzfeednews.com/article/annehelenpetersen/millennials-burnout-generation-debt-work

[19] Jackson, Ashton. "Millennial managers are more burned out than any other generation." CNBC makeit. December 22, 2021. https://www.cnbc.com/2021/12/22/millennial-managers-are-more-burned-out-than-any-other-generation.html

[20] Petersen, Anne Helen, "How Millennials Became the Burnout Generation." BuzzFeed, January 5, 2019. https://www.buzzfeednews.com/article/annehelenpetersen/millennials-burnout-generation-debt-work

[21] Nicol-Schwarz, Kai. "Burnout and bullying: Why startup workers' mental health is so bad." Sifted. August 17, 2022. https://sifted.eu/articles/mental-health-workplace/

[22] Axonify, "Annual Global State of Frontline Work Experience," October 14, 2021, https://www.prnewswire.com/news-releases/axonify-releases-annual-global-state-of-frontline-work-experience-study-301399564.html

[23] Hazell, Cassie. 'You have to suffer for your PhD': poor mental health among doctoral researchers – new research." *The Conversation*. January 11, 2022. https://theconversation.com/you-have-to-suffer-for-your-phd-poor-mental-health-among-doctoral-researchers-new-research-174096

[24] Brower, Tracy. "Nearly 70% of people work on vacation." Forbes. July 17, 2022. https://www.forbes.com/sites/tracybrower/2022/07/17/nearly-70-of-people-work-on-vacation-7-ways-to-detach/?sh=1200c34f2a69

[25] Gura, David. "'Absolute Meltdown': Wall Street's Work Till You Drop Culture Under Attack." NPR. May 7, 2021.

https://www.npr.org/2021/05/07/993938573/absolute-meltdown-wall-streets-work-till-you-drop-culture-under-attack#:~:text=work%20on%20Saturdays.-,Burnout%20in%20investment%20banking%20has%20been%20a%20problem%2C%20but%20the,%2C%2024%20hours%20a%20day.%22

26 Mayo Clinic, "Job burnout: How to spot it and take action," accessed November 1, 2022, https://www.mayoclinic.org/healthy-lifestyle/adult-health/in-depth/burnout/art-20046642

27 Reid, Penny. "Penny Reid Quotes," accessed November 27, 2022, https://www.goodreads.com/quotes/8759153-don-t-set-yourself-on-fire-trying-to-keep-others-warm

28 Tyler, Mara. "When work becomes an addiction." Healthline. December 19, 2017. https://www.healthline.com/health/addiction/work#:~:text=Work%20addiction%2C%20often%20called%20workaholism,often%20driven%20by%20job%20success

29 Conley, Chip. *Emotional Equations* (New York: Atria Paperback, 2012).

30 Minkoff, R. and Allers, R. (Directors). (1994). *The Lion King* (Film). Disney Productions.

31 Godin, Seth. *The Dip* (New York: Portfolio Publishing / Penguin Group, 2007).

32 Godin, Seth. *The Dip* (New York: Portfolio Publishing / Penguin Group, 2007).

33 Dalton-Smith, Dr. Saundra, *Sacred Rest: Recover Your Life, Renew Your Energy, Restore Your Sanity* (Tennessee: FaithWords, 2017)

34 Sullivan, Sandy. The Alchemy Group. https://www.thealchemyleaders.com/

35 Wayfinders Collective, "Stepping Forward Into Growth," accessed Oct 17, 2022, https://www.wayfinderscollective.com/get-inspired/2017/11/29/stepping-forward-into-

growth#:~:text=Abraham%20Maslow%20said%2C%20%E2%80%9CIn%20any,to%20step%20forward%20into%20growth%3F

[36] Conley, Chip. *Emotional Equations* (New York: Atria Paperback, 2012).

[37] Johnson, Spencer, *Who Moved My Cheese?* (Simon & Schuste, 2009).

[38] Goodreads, "Theodore Roosevelt Quotes," accessed November 17, 2022, https://www.goodreads.com/quotes/7-it-is-not-the-critic-who-counts-not-the-man

[39] Lynkova, Darina. "How Many Emails Are Sent Per Day in 2022?" techjury. November 26, 2022. https://techjury.net/blog/how-many-emails-are-sent-per-day/#gref

[40] Anwar, Yasmin. "How Many Different Human Emotions Are There?" Berkeley University of California. September 8, 2017. https://greatergood.berkeley.edu/article/item/how_many_different_human_emotions_are_there

[41] Robbins, Anthony. *Awaken the Giant Within* (New York: Free Press, 1991)

[42] Carroll, Lewis, "If you don't know where you are going, any road will take you there," accessed 12-1-22, https://www.brainyquote.com/quotes/lewis_carroll_165865

[43] Philips, Alan. "A Great Man (or Woman) is a Sentence." Medium. January 23, 2019. https://medium.com/@alan_46156/a-great-man-or-woman-is-a-sentence-45b463ba0fa9

[44] Piper, John. *Don't Waste Your Life*. Light and Heat National Conference: A Passion for the Holiness of God, 2011.

[45] Sullivan, Sandy. Source: Personal conversation, 2017.

[46] Belle-Isle, Linda and David. inColor inSight. https://incolorinsight.com/

[47] Csikszentmihalyui, Mihali. *Flow: The Psychology of Optimal Experience (New York: Harper Collins Publishers, 2008).*

[48] Conley, Chip. *Emotional Equations* (New York: Atria Paperback, 2012).

[49] Conley, Chip. *Emotional Equations* (New York: Atria Paperback, 2012).

[50] Csikszentmihalyui, Mihali. *Flow: The Psychology of Optimal Experience (New York: Harper Collins Publishers, 2008).*

[51] Brown, Brené. *The Gifts of Imperfection* (Minnesota: Hazelden Publishing, 2010).

[52] Newton, Claire. "The Rocks and Pebbles Sand Story." Accessed December 1, 2022. https://www.clairenewton.co.za/my-articles/the-rocks-pebbles-and-sand-story.html

[53] Matthew 6:22 (World English Bible).

[54] Versant Health, "15 Facts About All Things Eyes," accessed November 9, 2022, https://versanthealth.com/blog/15-facts-about-all-things-eyes/

[55] "Sparkle," Collier's Dictionary. https://www.collinsdictionary.com/us/dictionary/english/collier. Accessed Dec 6, 2022.

[56] Brown, Brené. *The Gifts of Imperfection* (Minnesota: Hazelden Publishing, 2010).

[57] Kubler-Ross, Elisabeth, "People are like stained glass windows." https://mindzip.net/fl/@ElisabethKubler-Ross/quotes/people-are-like-stained-glass-windows-they-sparkle-and-shine-when-the-sun-is-out-but-when-the-darkness-sets-in-their-true-beauty-is-revealed-only-if-there-is-a-light-from-

within-558a9027-1a49-4fe2-9076-ec220c0d3e4a.

[58] DDI, "57 Percent of Employees Quit Because of Their Boss," accessed Nov 20, 2022, https://www.prnewswire.com/news-releases/new-ddi-research-57-percent-of-employees-quit-because-of-their-boss-300971506.html

[59] DDI, "57 Percent of Employees Quit Because of Their Boss," accessed Nov 20, 2022, https://www.prnewswire.com/news-releases/new-ddi-research-57-percent-of-employees-quit-because-of-their-boss-300971506.html

[60] Matthew 7:5 (World English Bible).

[61] Haynes, A. (2005). Buddha. Vertical.

[62] Kasil, Stanislav and Slade, Martin. "Thinking Positively About Aging Extends Life More than Exercise and Not Smoking." Yale News. July 29, 2022. https://news.yale.edu/2002/07/29/thinking-positively-about-aging-extends-life-more-exercise-and-not-smoking

[63] Castrillon, Caroline. "5 Ways To Go From A Scarcity To Abundance Mindset." Forbes. July 12, 2020. https://www.forbes.com/sites/carolinecastrillon/2020/07/12/5-ways-to-go-from-a-scarcity-to-abundance-mindset/?sh=5b8aa6131197

[64] Zander, Rosamund. *The Art of Possibility* (New York: Penguin Books, 2002).

[65] Clarity Clinic, "The Cherokee Two Wolves Story and the Power of Mindset," October 15, 2020, https://www.claritychi.com/the-cherokee-two-wolves-story-and-the-power-of-mindset/

[66] Haynes, A. (2005). Buddha. Vertical.

[67] Hargrove, Robert. *Masterful Coaching* (New Jersey: Pfeiffer Publishing, 2008).

[68] Chandler Coaches, "Are You Telling Yourself Rut Stories or River Stories?"

October 12, 2010, https://chandlercoaches.com/are-you-telling-yourself-rut-stories-or-river-stories/

[69] Chandler Coaches, "Are You Telling Yourself Rut Stories or River Stories?" October 12, 2010, https://chandlercoaches.com/are-you-telling-yourself-rut-stories-or-river-stories/

[70] Goldsmith, Marshall. *Majo: How to Get It, How to Keep It, How to Get it Back if You Lose It* (New York: Hachette Books, 2009).

[71] Goodreads, "Clive Cussler Quotes," accessed November 17, 2022, https://www.goodreads.com/quotes/7275603-time-is-a-thief-it-steals-our-memory-our-hopes

[72] New York Times, "Parental Burnout Symptoms," May 5, 2022, https://www.nytimes.com/2022/05/05/well/family/parental-burnout-symptoms.html

[73] Goss, Tracy. *The Last Word on Power* (New York: Rosetta Books, 2010).

[74] Extraordinary Advisors, "Banish Your Itty Bitty Shitty Committee", accessed October 17, 2022, https://extraordinaryadvisors.com/banish-your-itty-bitty-shitty-committee/

[75] Brown, Brené. *The Gifts of Imperfection* (Minnesota: Hazelden Publishing, 2010).

[76] Brown, Brené. *The Gifts of Imperfection* (Minnesota: Hazelden Publishing, 2010).

[77] Brown, Brené. *The Gifts of Imperfection* (Minnesota: Hazelden Publishing, 2010).

[78] Dalton-Smith, Dr. Saundra, *Sacred Rest: Recover Your Life, Renew Your Energy, Restore Your Sanity* (Tennessee: FaithWords, 2017)

[79] Sleep Foundation, "Sleep Statistics," accessed November 2, 2022, https://www.sleepfoundation.org/how-sleep-works/sleep-facts-statistics

[80] *Web*Md, "What are REM and Non-REM Sleep?" November 15,2022, https://www.webmd.com/sleep-disorders/sleep-101

[81] Dalton-Smith, Dr. Saundra, *Sacred Rest: Recover Your Life, Renew Your Energy, Restore Your Sanity* (Tennessee: FaithWords, 2017)

[82] Harvard Graduate School, "Loneliness in America: How the Pandemic Has Deepened an Epidemic of Loneliness and What We Can Do About It," accessed November 16, 2022, "https://mcc.gse.harvard.edu/reports/loneliness-in-america

[83] Harvard Graduate School, "Loneliness in America: How the Pandemic Has Deepened an Epidemic of Loneliness and What We Can Do About It," accessed November 16, 2022, "https://mcc.gse.harvard.edu/reports/loneliness-in-america

[84] Healthline, "What Does It Mean to Be Touch Starved?", accessed November 19, 2022, https://www.healthline.com/health/touch-starved#signs-to-watch

[85] Harvard Graduate School, "Loneliness in America: How the Pandemic Has Deepened an Epidemic of Loneliness and What We Can Do About It," accessed November 16, 2022, https://mcc.gse.harvard.edu/reports/loneliness-in-america

[86] Robbins, Anthony. *Awaken the Giant Within* (New York: Free Press, 1991)

[87] Thompson, Gregg and Biro, Susanne. *Unleashed! Leader as Coach* (New York: SelectBooks, Inc. 2006).

[88] Doyle, Glenna, *Untamed* (New York City: The Dial Press, 2020).

[89] Goodreads, "Dan Pena Quotes," accessed November 17, 2022, https://www.goodreads.com/quotes/10834469-show-me-your-friends-and-i-ll-show-you-your-future

[90] Robbins, Anthony. *Awaken the Giant Within* (New York: Free Press, 1991)

[91] Godin, Seth. *The Dip* (New York: Portfolio Publishing / Penguin Group, 2007).

[92] Rohn, Jim. "Jim Rohn quotes". Accessed November 21, 2022. https://www.goodreads.com/quotes/1798-you-are-the-average-of-the-five-people-you-spend.

[93] Dalton-Smith, Dr. Saundra, *Sacred Rest: Recover Your Life, Renew Your Energy, Restore Your Sanity* (Tennessee: FaithWords, 2017)

[94] Matthew 11:28-29 (World English Bible).

[95] Philippians 4:7 (World English Bible).

[96] Exodus 33:14 (World English Bible).

[97] Psalm 23 (World English Bible).

[98] John 16:33 (World English Bible).

[99] Strobel, Lee. *The Case for Christ* (New York: Zondervan, 1998).

[100] Burke, John. *Imagine Heaven* (Michigan: Baker Books, 2015).

[101] Burke, John. *Imagine Heaven* (Michigan: Baker Books, 2015).

www.ingramcontent.com/pod-product-compliance
Lightning Source LLC
LaVergne TN
LVHW051227080426
835513LV00016B/1455